MANAGEMENT EDUCATION:
AN INTERNATIONAL SURVEY

Management Education
An International Survey

EDITED BY WILLIAM BYRT

R

ROUTLEDGE
London and New York

First published 1989
by Routledge
11 New Fetter Lane, London EC4P 4EE
29 West 35th Street, New York NY 10001

© 1989 William Byrt

Printed in Great Britain by
Billing & Sons Ltd, Worcester

British Library Cataloguing in Publication Data
Management education.
    Educational institutions. Curriculum
    subjects. Management
    I. Byrt, W.J.
    658'.007'11

Library of Congress Cataloging-in-Publication Data
Management education.

    Includes index.
    1. Management — Study and teaching. I. Byrt. W.J.
(William John)
HD30.4.M33 1988 658'.007   88-26353
ISBN 0-415-00423-2

CONTENTS

ACKNOWLEDGEMENTS

Each of the contributors acknowledges the help of a large number of people who contributed to this research. The list is too long to reproduce in full but their valuable assistance is gratefully acknowledged.

Special thanks is due to Ros Dawson-Marsh of the Graduate School of Management in the University of Melbourne who performed the onerous and exacting task of producing the camera-ready copy of the book.

CONTRIBUTORS

Bernard Barry is Professor of Organisational Behaviour at the Cranfield School of Management. He was previously Professor of Business Administration in the Graduate School of Management at the University of Melbourne (1981-1984) and Director of Research at Ashridge Management College (1970-1981). He is currently a member of the Education Committee of the Institute of Directors; a member of a number of editorial boards and an External Examiner for Trinity College, Dublin, the University of Glasgow and Leicester Polytechnic.

Jean-Louis Barsoux graduated with Honours in Business Administration with a Foreign Language from Loughborough University in 1984. Following a year's national service in France he is now in the process of completing a doctoral thesis on the character of French management and is co-author with Peter Lawrence of a forthcoming book on French management.

John Blake is Lecturer in Financial Accounting in the Department of Management Studies, Loughborough University. He is author of six books and over twenty articles on Accounting, Management and Small Business.

William Byrt is currently a senior Associate in the Graduate School of Management in the University of Melbourne. He was previously Reader and Acting Professor in the Graduate School of Business Administration of that University. He is the author of about fifty articles and a dozen books on Organisation Theory and Behaviour, Management and Business-Government Relations. He has spent periods as Visiting Professor at the University of the Witwatersrand and Cranfield School of Management and Visiting Fellow at Henley: the Management School.

Kevin Collins is a lecturer in the Centre for Comparative and International Studies in Education in the School of Education at La Trobe University. He has written a variety of papers on different aspects of Japanese education, including such areas as Vocational Training, Education as a Preparation for, and During Employment, and Comparative Educational Statistics. Research currently underway is directed at Skill Formation.

Peter Lawrence is Senior Lecturer in the Department of Management Studies, University of Loughborough. He previously worked at the Universities of Strathclyde and Southampton and has held visiting professorships/research fellowships in West Germany, East Germany, France, Sweden, the Netherlands and Israel. His major research work is in the fields of the engineering dimension in the national economy, comparative management, and in the nature of management work.

Jack F McKenna received his PhD from the University of California, Irvine Campus in 1978 and is currently a Professor of Management in the College of Business at California State University, Chico. He has published over sixty articles and conference papers in the areas of Human Resource Administration, Organisational Growth and Occupational Stress. Additionally, he has authored two books and has made chapter contributions to six others.

Chapter One

MANAGEMENT EDUCATION
William Byrt

First, what is management? Sometimes distinctions
are made between management and administration.
However, these distinctions vary. In some cases,
administration is regarded as the higher and
management as the lower level activity. In others
the opposite view is taken, management is regarded
as a higher-level activity than is administration.

In the past, particularly in Britain and in
some of the nations which evolved from the British
Empire, administration has been considered as an
activity carried out in the public sector; a common
division of government functions being into executive, legislative, administrative and judicial. A
similar activity in the private sector being termed
management. In both Britain and Australia there are
Royal Institutes of Public Administration and
Institutes of Management. The former concentrate on
the public sector and, although the latter include
members, both corporate and individual, from the
public sector, their emphasis is on private
industry.

Today, there is a tendency to treat the two
terms as being synonymous. The original Mecca of
management education, the Harvard Business School,
has as its official title that of Graduate School
of Business Administration. Harvard, of course,
also houses the John F Kennedy School of Public
Administration.

In Britain, courses leading to degrees of
Master of Business Administration are offered by
the London and Manchester Graduate Schools of
Business Administration and by the Cranfield School
of Management. In Australia, similar courses are

1

offered by the Australian Graduate School of Management in the University of New South Wales and by the Graduate School of Management in the University of Melbourne.

These are only examples. Around the world there are many variations in the titles of management degrees offered and the schools offering them. The most satisfactory practice would appear to be to designate as 'management' the subject with which we are concerned. The term administration may be treated as being synonymous with management or, as I do later, as covering a certain class of operational as distinct from managerial work.

We are still left with the problem of defining management. Different writers define it in different ways; Urwick stated that he had collected more than twenty definitions, not always consistent. Some do not bother to define the term, assuming that the reader will know what is meant by it or that the meaning will become apparent from what is written. One is tempted to state that 'management is what managers do', excepting that, usually, not all the management of any organisation is performed entirely by persons designated as managers. It may be carried out, for example, by engineers, lawyers, accountants, medicos, salesmen, foremen - or even judges. Also, different managers do different things, perform different functions and play different roles.

Does it matter whether or not the term is defined if those performing the function are clear as to what they are doing? It probably does matter. Definition may structure, even determine, an argument or discussion whether it be in management, politics, economics or religion. Definition aids power. An over-quoted statement from Lewis Carroll's _Through the Looking Glass_ is Humpty Dumpty's: 'When I use a word, it means just what I choose it to mean - neither more nor less'. Not so well-known is the ensuing dialogue:

> "The question is", said Alice, "whether you _can_ make words mean so many different things".
> "The question is", said Humpty Dumpty, "which is to be master - that's all."

The skillful dialectician, politician, teacher - or manager - can structure a discussion according to how he or she is permitted to define the major terms.

"First come I, my name is Jowett,
There is no knowledge but I know it.
I am the Master of this College,
What I don't know isn't knowledge."
            ("The Masque of Balliol")

Let me start with my definition of management:

"Management is the process through which
an organisation's strategy is formulated
and then implemented through the
organisation of work, people, finance and
technology."

STRATEGY

An organisation's strategy consists of <u>what</u> and <u>how</u>
over the long term: what its objectives are, how
they are to be achieved through the utilisation of
human, financial and technological resources. One
can probably also add <u>why</u>: why these objectives and
why do we intend to pursue them in this fashion?
The overall strategy of an organisation is usually
termed corporate and is developed from a number of
sub-strategies: development; production; marketing
- the development of goods and services, their
production and their marketing. Also, there may be
sub-strategies as to means: personnel, financial
and technological.
    The process of strategy formulation, or
strategic planning, is illustrated in Figure 1.1.

Information

Planning, the process of making plans and monitoring and revising them, is based on information.
Information may be transmitted in writing, through
words, numbers, symbols and illustrations. It may
also be transmitted orally or through actions. It
may be received by reading, listening or through
observation. Management information may be stored
in records, computerised or non-computerised, or in
people's minds as a result of education, training,
experience or socialisation.
    Many organisations have suffered from a paucity
of vital information or from getting it too late to
take action or in a form of little use to management. Today it is recognised that management information is vital to the operation of an organisation

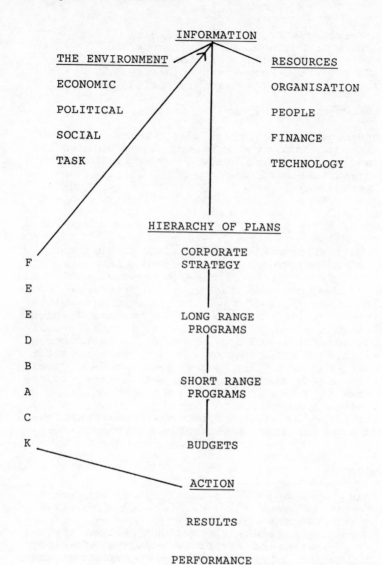

STRATEGIC PLANNING

FIGURE 1.1

and the collection, presentation and analysis of such information has been revolutionised through the use of computers.

In formulating strategy, managers must look outside the organisation at the environment and inside at the organisation's resources, actual and potential.

The environment

An organisation's, economic, political and social environments may be local - community, city or state - national or international.

Its task environment consists of the individuals and groups with which it is in close contact: its markets, its suppliers of people, finance and technology, trade unions and government agencies.

Its markets being made up of the consumers, or potential consumers, of the goods and services which it produces or may produce expressed in terms of their needs and their desire and ability to satisfy those needs.

An essential part of strategic planning is analysing the relevant parts of the environment, forecasting movements in it and monitoring it during the period in which the plan is to be implemented. A good deal of environmental analysis, particularly in large organisations, is carried out by specialist groups: corporate planners; economists; corporate affairs groups; market and technological researchers. However, any manager needs to be sensitive to the state of the environment and may be required to make some input into the planning process in the form of information, advice, opinions or decisions.

Resources

Planning requires that an assessment be made of an organisation's resources: organisational; people; finance; technology.

What is the nature of the organisation structure; the systems of authority and communication, the allocation of work, the work processes and methods? Are these appropriate for the strategy to be pursued? Should they and could they be changed?

What sorts of people staff the organisation? What are their ages, personal characteristics, skills and abilities? Are they appropriate for implementing the strategy? If not, can they be trained, replaced or supplemented?

What is the financial situation of the organisation? Its capital structure, source of funds, cash flow? Again, is it adequate or can it be supplemented in any way?

A similar type of analysis may be made of technology which may consist of things, such as equipment, such as wordprocessors, activities, knowledge, such as formulae and theories.

The Hierarchy of Plans

Plans are formulated as the result of the analysis of the external environment and of internal resources. The plans of an organisation form a hierarchy becoming more specific and covering a shorter term as they proceed from corporate strategy, through long-range programs, to short-range ones.

Action

Strategy is implemented through action. The management of strategy implementation is the aspect of management on which writers usually concentrate. However, results and performance depend a good deal on the planning that precedes them. One of the early theorists of management, Peter Drucker, termed, as a blind spot, the divorce of planning from doing:

'Planning and doing are separate parts of the same job; they are not separate jobs.'(1)

Feedback

Plans do not achieve themselves. Action needs to be monitored, performance being compared with plan. The results of this monitoring should be fed-back so that the analysis of data and plans may be kept under constant review and revised if necessary. Monitoring may be carried out through reports, computerised and non-computerised, records, observation and discussion.

THE IMPLEMENTATION OF STRATEGY

Strategy is implemented through the design of organisation structures and the management of work, people, money and technology.

Structural Design

Most exercises in structural design entail modifying or adding to existing structures. If we examine any organisation we will usually find that its structure has evolved over time. Starting, perhaps, with a small, even one-person, organisation and being built-on until it reaches its present state.

Some exercises in structural design start, of course, from the ground up. A new structure, either for the organisation as a whole or for part of it, being designed.

Structural design entails:

Formulation of strategies.
Tracing work-flows.
Job construction.
Departmentation.
Establishment of relationships between
  jobs and between the occupants of those jobs.

The Management of Work

Work is, of course, largely managed by setting up an appropriate organisation structure and by managing people, money and technology. However, the work process itself needs to be managed. This entails:

Designing work processes
Determining work methods
Setting standards and targets
Monitoring performance.

Work processes

A work process may be considered as a pipe-line along which goods or services flow, starting with the raw material, which may consist of actual materials such as bricks, metals or fluids or of intangibles such as needs, ideas, orders or requests, and ending with the completed goods or services.

The factory production line is the most obvious example of this sort of work process although most processes, even for professional services, resemble it. Most work processes set up problems of interrelationships. It is seldom that one person is responsible for the whole process from beginning to end, particularly in complex processes. Timing, quality, quantity, certainty and uncertainty and co-operativeness are all of prime importance.

7

Work methods

The methods of carrying out particular work may be arrived at in a variety of ways:

Custom: This is the way it has always been done.

Bureaucratic Rules: In bureaucracies it is common to have work methods laid down by some superior authority. This is a means of ensuring uniformity of treatment, predictability and fairness.

Work Study: The work is analysed and the 'best' method of doing it determined.

The Informal Organisation: One aspect of the informal organisation is to permit individuals and groups a fair amount of freedom in determining how their work should be done.

Standards and targets

Standards and targets, the quality and quantity of work to be performed in a certain time, may also be set in different ways: custom; bureaucratic rules; work study; the informal organisation, e.g. 'dargs' or unofficial quotas.

Standards are usually expressed specifically in terms of production figures and, generally, in terms of effectiveness and efficiency. Effectiveness being the extent to which objectives are met, efficiency the ratio of output to inputs of labour, money, materials and technology.

Monitoring performance

As pointed out earlier, performance may be monitored through reports, records, observations and discussion.

The Management of People

The term human resource management appears to have replaced that of personnel management. Whatever term is used, the management of people in medium and large-sized organisations is usually shared between staff specialists, usually entitled human resource or personnel managers, and the managers, sometimes referred to as line managers, to whom the people are responsible for the performance of their work. Managers manage people according to their own styles and in accordance with various laws, awards, rules and policies.

The way in which the function of human resource management is divided between specialists and line managers varies from organisation to organisation. In some cases, the specialists perform a purely lateral or staff function, providing service, advice, auditing, co-ordination and research and development. In others, they may also perform direct managerial functions such as recruitment, selection, dismissal, counselling. No matter what division of functions is made, the line manager has direct responsibility for the management of the people reporting to him or her and should be involved, as far as possible, even in the activities performed by the specialists.

The management of people may be illustrated by considering people, in their employment by an organisation, as passing along a pipe-line with three major parts:

> Entry
> Career
> Termination.

Entry

The staffing requirements of an organisation need to be planned in terms of numbers and types required and timing of employment. This involves:

> Recruitment
> Selection
> Employment
> Induction
> Placement.

Career

This is the period during which the employee carries out the work allotted to him or her. The main matters involved in managing people during this period are:

> Allocation of work
> Monitoring performance
> Supervision of activities
> Appraisal of people
> Training and development
> Career Progression
> Counselling
> Grievances
> Remuneration
> Safety, Health and Welfare
> Employee-Involvement in Management

Group Dynamics
Management-Union Relationships.

Termination

Termination of employment may be due to death, retirement, resignation, retrenchment or dismissal. The conditions of termination are usually governed, to a great extent, by legislation, awards, rules or policy. Also, in medium and large organisations, specialists may, to a great extent, handle terminations.

However, line managers may be involved in some cases, particularly in deciding or recommending retrenchment or dismissal or in counselling or advising leavers or potential leavers.

The Management of Money

Traditionally, there has been a tendency in medium and large-sized organisations to leave financial management to specialists, principally accountants. However, in recent years there has been a move to involve other managers in it, not only in providing inputs of information and opinions to assist in the compilation of financial plans but in the management of such plans; in effect making them accountable for the financial management of their own areas of responsibility.

This move has been facilitated by creating a hierarchy of financial plans or budgets, starting with the corporate plan and coming down through divisional, branch, sectional and program budgets. Through budgeting, the costs of organisations and sections of them and of programs can be determined. Performance can then be measured by comparing what has been achieved with budgeted costs. Particular managers can be made responsible for achieving budget, ranging from the corporate one to that for a particular program.

It is, then, desirable that most managers should have some knowledge and understanding of accountancy and of financial management. It is not enough to accept a budget, attempt to work within it but to ask for extra funds if it is not possible to do so. The manager needs to be able to engage in 'financial housekeeping'; not only to contribute to the compilation of the budget but to manipulate it in order to achieve optimum performance.

The Management of Technology

Technology consists of the things, activities and knowledge by means of which work is carried out. Managers should understand the technology appropriate to the work which they manage. They should be able to utilise it; not necessarily operate the things or perform the activities. They need to understand the relevant knowledge and, where possible, develop various aspects of technology.

A major technological development in recent years has been computerisation. Managers need not be able to program or operate a computer. They should, however, be aware of what can be achieved through computerisation and be able to utilise computers either through their own or specialist staff.

THE DEVELOPMENT OF MANAGERS

There are two major classes of work, operational and managerial. Operational work is also termed, in some cases and according to its nature, technical or professional. Operational work entails the direct production or contribution to production of goods and services, wholly or in part: adjusting a machine; drafting a contract; delivering a judgment; writing a report; selling an article; analysing financial statements. A definition of management or managerial work was given earlier.

There are four main classes of jobs:

Operational: containing no appreciable managerial element, e.g. the work of a fitter; surgeon; barrister; production worker; salesperson.

Operational/Managerial: principally operational but with a managerial component, e.g. leading hand; supervisor.

Managerial/Operational: principally managerial but with an operational component, e.g. most middle and senior management.

Managerial: containing no appreciable operational element, e.g. chief executives.

Methods of performing most forms of operational work are fairly clear-cut, being determined by custom, experience, training, awards, legislation or policies. They are learned through experience or through on-the-job or classroom training. However, the methods of performing managerial work are not so clear-cut. Such work is made up of a diversity of functions and what one manager does may bear little relationship to what is done by another.

From time-to-time, we have bodies, such as Institutes of Management, floating the idea that management should be recognised as a profession. However, the hallmarks of a profession are standard qualifications and conditions of entry into it, standard methods of training and codes of ethics and behaviour. It is most unlikely that such characteristics could be identified for the occupation of management. There is even debate as to whether the practice of management constitutes an art or a skill.

The peculiar nature of management presents some difficulties for those who, recognising its importance and the need for organisations to be managed effectively and efficiently, desire to develop principles of management and methods of training and educating managers.

The early writers on management, those writing during the first quarter of this century, attempted to develop such principles. Many of these writers were engineers and considered that, as principles and laws had been developed for disciplines such as engineering and chemistry, they could also be developed for management. Principles being defined as fundamental truths, such truths being descriptive, prescriptive or normative. The most widely-accepted principles were concerned with the structuring and operation of organisations and have been termed, variously, principles of management, administration or organisation. For example:

Administrative **efficiency** is increased by specialisation of the task among the group.
Administrative **efficiency** is enhanced by arranging the members of an organisation in a determinate hierarchy of authority in order to preserve unity of command.
Administrative **efficiency** is enhanced by limiting the number of subordinates whose work is interrelated and who report to one manager to a small number - say six.

These principles formed the basis of what was regarded as 'good' management and of various training and education courses in management or supervision. During the 1930s they came under fire from members of the behavioural school of management theorists who contended that the so-called principles did not constitute fundamental truths. The approach of the classical theorists, who had developed the principles, was criticised as being mechanistic. The behaviouralists, in their research and observations, discerned a good deal of working behaviour as being contingent or relative, even non-rational. The most influential attack on the principles was made in 1945 by Herbert Simon.(2)

Today, writers on and teachers of management and managers find some of the principles of value as statements against which to test practice. However, they are not regarded as fundamental truths but as propositions which are valid under certain conditions but not under others.

The contingency approach in management theory is generally accepted: 'It all depends'. Most writers, teachers and practitioners agree, in general, that organisations in which management is carried out constitute open systems. The results of managerial decisions depend, to a great extent, on the environment in which they are made and the interrelationships between the components of the organisation: people, structure, strategy and technology.

Despite the widespread acceptance of contingency theory, there is general belief that the results of experience in, perception of and research into management in situations other than the manager's own <u>can</u> be of value to him or her. Wisdom, knowledge and skill are transferable, through writings, lectures, discussions and case-studies, provided that their results are not applied mechanistically as precepts, rules or dogma but rather as propositions or insights. To some extent, management can be taught.

Given that the skills and experience of managers can be supplemented by training and education, what form should such training and education take? Again: 'it all depends'.

If the earlier description of the nature of management is accepted, it would appear that an organisation needs managers who can carry out the following tasks:

> Environmental Analysis
> Resource Analysis
> Organisation Design
> Job Design
> Management of Information Systems
> Human Resource Management

Financial Management
Management of Technology

A management development program should, then, cover these areas. Each may, of course, be broken down into sub-areas and it is here that debate begins. Should a particular program, whether award (degree, diploma or certificate) or non-award contain this or that subject?

There is a lack of clarity as to the purpose of management education. First, is its principal purpose to educate or to train managers? Secondly, at what groups is it directed and what are the educators attempting to achieve with each group?

Most management educators, at least those in tertiary institutions, would claim that their principal task was to provide education: to widen the horizons, conceptually, environmentally and emotionally, of their pupils; to develop their analytical abilities; to facilitate their self-awareness. However, many of those undertaking management education courses are looking for training. They seek to be taught specific skills.

The distinction between education and training is at the heart of the matter of the content of management education courses. Should such courses be general or specific? Should they provide the student with a wide or narrow choice of subjects? Should they be 'hard' or 'soft'? Should they include these subjects or those?

It is also central to the question of what is expected of management education. Is it expected to produce general managers or skilled technicians?

Some management education courses are training courses, no matter what title is given to them. Most constitute a mixture of education and training. But where is the emphasis? What are the expectations of those undertaking the courses or of the organisations sponsoring them?

A good deal of education of any kind constitutes an act of faith and management education is probably no more such an act than are many other widely accepted forms. It may be claimed that the input to a system of education is less important than the output, what the graduates do on graduation and what use they make of the results of that education. The British Empire was developed by persons educated largely in the humanities at Oxford and Cambridge, supported by a myriad of highly-motivated, lesser functionaries, both expatriate and indigenous, trained in a narrow range of skills. It is important that students of management should be given an opportunity to reflect on their experiences and to share them with others. However, it is desirable that there should be a structure, a course, within which such experiential learning should take place.

There is a great deal of diversity among managerial jobs and yet there are similarities. There are two extreme points of view:

"We're different." Each organisation is unique in its managerial functions and in the skills and abilities required of its managers.

"Management is management, is management." The functions to be performed by managers and the skills and abilities required of them are the same in any organisation.

The truth probably lies between the two extremes. Different organisations may have quite different managerial requirements. A manager who has been successful in one organisation may be a failure in another. Practices, procedures and policies which have succeeded in one may fail when adopted elsewhere.

Yet there are similarities between the managerial functions of different organisations. Successful managers in particular organisations have transferred to become successful in quite different ones.

Management is a complex subject. Different managers do different things and the skills, abilities and functions of critical importance in some management jobs may be quite different from those of importance in others.

However, the quality of management in organisations has such a vital bearing on our economic, social and personal lives that it cannot be allowed to depend on chance; on managers learning to manage entirely through practice, 'picking-up' skills as they go along. Today, most organisations engage in some form of management development. Even those who rely heavily on filling their key management positions by buying them from other organisations, are benefiting from management development carried out by others.

Management development entails developing various skills of persons so that they are better able to meet the needs of organisations for efficient and effective management and to satisfy the self-actualisation needs of those being developed. So that management development programs seek to satisfy the needs of two parties: employing organisations and managers; to which may be added a third, educational institutions.

Management development may be carried out through three means: experience; training; education. The approaches to training and education adopted in a number of countries are outlined in the chapters that follow.

NOTES

1.   Peter   F.   Drucker,   <u>The   Practice   of Management</u>, Mercury Books, London, 1961, p.251.
2.   Herbert A. Simon, <u>Administrative Behavior</u>, The Free Press, New York, 1976.

Chapter Two

MANAGEMENT EDUCATION IN THE UNITED STATES
Jack F. McKenna

An education in business administration can mean a
number of quite divergent things depending on the
context in which it is discussed. Political,
geographical, social and temporal factors all have
the potential to significantly influence what is
meant by a higher education in business. While the
United States certainly cannot claim to be the
first country in the world to educate its
population in the importance of business, it has
well been recognised as a world leader in research
and education in matters pertaining to business and
management.

It is the intention of this chapter to
introduce the reader to what has been, and is
currently meant by higher education in business
administration in America. It is important to note
that the current state of business education in the
US has evolved from a number of significant and
interrelated developments dating most specifically
from the period just prior to the Industrial
Revolution in America. Keeping this in mind, the
introductory portion of this chapter will explore
the foundations of higher education in business in
the United States, the economic and social issues
which shaped business education, and the outcomes
which were produced.

After this introduction we will turn our attention to those issues and forces which currently
mold the character and set the stage for business
education in the later part of the 20th century in
the US. Finally, in the concluding section of this
chapter we will search for recommendation regarding
what should be done to keep American business

education effectively positioned in the world economic community and serving the needs of both domestic and foreign students.

A COUNTRY OF BUSINESS

Even the most casual observer of US social/ cultural practices would be quick to recognise that American business shoulders a considerable burden. The very roots of our relatively young country are commercial. As a British colony our country was exploited for its agricultural, mineral and intellectual resources and, as a newly formed sovereign state, commerce was to bear the load of its future development.

While there is little question that US commerce and industry have made our country into a significant economic and scientific force in a world society, the question still remains as to how it was so successfully accomplished. Certainly one of the primary forces in the rapid development of American business has been the education of our society in general and higher education in business in particular.

The educational foundation of the US society is a unique one by world standards. Never before had a country set out with such ambitious educational objectives. As an important component of the American democratic plan it was viewed as absolutely essential that all members of society should be provided with the right of a free education. Although it would certainly be inaccurate to suggest that this country has been completely successful in achieving its educational objectives, it has made considerable progress in its 200-plus year history.

Although business education is relatively new on the academic scene, members of our society have been trained in the economic and business practices of living, for generations and from birth. Every parent recognises the significant role that economic activity plays in the development of his or her children and will, almost without notice, begin at an early age developing business intellectual skills in these new members of society. Early interactions with playmates and teachers only serve to further develop and refine the business talents of US youth. So it is possible to see that, long before a college or university student elects to pursue a degree track in business administration

19

and ultimately a career in public accounting, finance, or management, his or her training in commerce has been extensive.

Business education, or what may be referred to in many countries as management education, was given birth in the US in a substantially different form than we might find it today. Thus, it may be appropriate to suggest precisely what we mean by business education in the United States. In 1961 a national committee of recognised US educational professionals in business provided the following definition:

> That area of the educational process which concerns itself with vocational preparation for a business career or vocational and professional preparation for a career in teaching business, and also with business information important for every citizen and consumer in order that he may better understand and use his business and economic surroundings. (Delta Pi Epsilon, 1961: Business Education Terms Defined).

While it may be considerably easier to provide examples of business education than it would be to reach agreement as to what exactly it is, the above definition does seem to suggest its focus is two-fold: (1) to prepare individual members of society for future careers in business and (2) provide all members of the American society with relevant business and economic information.

Vocational Preparation

Preparing individual members of the US society for careers in business has always been the most pressing goal of business education in our country. From its early roots around the turn of the century much of this education and professional development took place at the secondary and vocational business school level. In these environments the young people of our society were prepared for careers in bookkeeping, typing, sales and various clerical functions. The focus here would be with technical business skills training in one or two year programs of study.

At the post secondary or college level the objective was to provide academic training for secondary school teachers who would ultimately be responsible for developing curricula and teaching classes in business skills.

In our society today, the responsibility for teaching business skills has been entirely assumed by secondary and private vocational schools as well as the community colleges. This has left the collegiate level business education with an opportunity to develop degree programs in a wide variety of professional level career tracks in industry and commerce.

General Education

Today, as well as historically, students at both the secondary and collegiate levels are required to take courses in economics and business. This is true regardless of whether or not they ultimately decide to pursue further formal education in business. Since the operations of independent businesses, both large and small, in our society play such a vital function it has long been recognised that all citizens should have an understanding of, and an appreciation for, business.

Within a general education, business education prepares US citizens in the areas of consumer education, the management of personal affairs, a general understanding of our economic society and common business skills such as typing, budgeting and record keeping. Courses focusing on these subjects are commonly taught in high schools, community colleges and adult education programs.

Continuing Education

We should also mention the importance of continuing education as part of the US business culture. Within the past several decades it has become all too obvious that an undergraduate or graduate education as a simple prerequisite for a career in business is not enough. Today's US businessmen and women must view an education in the general arena of business as a continuous adjunct to their careers.

This (typically non-degree) form of training and development in business may be offered by employers, trade associations, public and private universities and private consultants. The focus of these continuing educational efforts may be with developing expertise in technical areas such as computer applications, budgeting and management information systems. Alternatively, the objective may be to prepare managers, or potential managers, with improved administrative skills and practices. Regardless of program focus and delivery mode, the continuing education of today's managers and technical specialists remains one of the fastest growing areas of business education in the US today.

THE FOUNDATION OF BUSINESS EDUCATION

While it could be suggested that conscious and formal education directed toward business and commerce is an American invention,it is also well recognised that certain aspects of business such as commercial law and double-entry bookkeeping can be traced to the thirteenth and fourteenth centuries in Italy(1). However, even with this ambiguity regarding dates and places, there is little question that business education has been taken more seriously in the US than in any other country in the world. It is certainly safe to assume that the US has dedicated more resources over a longer period of time toward the preparation of its citizens for careers in business than other world societies.

The Apprenticeship System

While today a substantial portion of US education in business administration takes place on the college or university campus and is culminated with the awarding of an undergraduate or graduate degree, this has not always been the case. The earliest attempts directed toward vocational preparation in a world of commerce and industry would have to have been the American 'apprenticeship' system. This system was brought from Europe with the colonists and was simply a contract between the family of a young boy and a master craftsman. Under this obligation the boy would be indentured to the craftsman for a period of several years (typically seven) during which time the employer would be responsible for the maintenance of the indentured person. Typically such requirements as food, shelter, clothing, general education, and religious training would fall under the craftsman's obligations. Of course the major thrust of the indentured individual's training would be directed toward learning a skill or craft from which a career would develop.

It is not difficult to see that today's apprenticeship programs in skilled and semi-skilled labor unions have evolved from these earlier and much more basic roots. The objective is similar however. It is understood and accepted that an unskilled laborer must place him or herself into a particular, and many times today highly focused, training program under specific educational guidelines for a certain period of time. As the trainees become more skilled at their trade they will progress along a specific career path, become more highly valued and typically paid more for their work.

The Business College

Along with the Industrial Revolution in America came the need to expand training in the general arena of 'commerce'. The opportunities for individuals with basic skills in such areas as bookkeeping, typing, business math and accounting were numerous in the latter part of the 19th century and scores of business colleges sprang up in the eastern and mid-western portions of the United States.

These colleges of business were generally private and administered by teachers with minimum official credentials in commerce and education. Although these colleges were the first significant attempt to train large groups of individuals in the fundamentals of business administration, they grew quickly and served an important need as the Industrial Revolution took hold in the United States. For example, the Bryant and Stratton College of Business accepted its first class of students in 1853. From modest beginnings in Cleveland, within a decade fifty such schools existed through the nation(2).

Early Collegiate Level Business Education

The years around the turn of the century were quite significant for business education in the United States. It was during this period that the nation's first college level program in business education was started at Drixel Institute in Philadelphia (1898). At this time, collegiate level education in business administration seemed to be headed in two distinct directions. Universities and colleges were offering degree programs designed to meet the needs of the secondary teacher in business subjects as well as more advanced course work leading to preparation for careers in accountancy.

The newly created public high school focus on business education placed severe demands on the collegiate level for the preparation of secondary business teachers. The societal demands for individuals with professional business skills presented quite a challenge for the typical poorly qualified secondary teacher in business subjects. While these teachers might have been well trained in the business subjects which they were directed to teach, their professional background in education was minimal.

During this same period, roughly 1880-1915, the most prestigious tier of US universities were experimenting with the development of business programs and schools of business. In most instances, this focus on business administration evolved out of departments of economics which may have for some time been offering courses in business problems and behavior. For example, at the University of Chicago, the formation of the school of business (1898) developed out of a set of courses offered by the Department of Political Economy. Such courses as Money and Banking, Transportation and Practical Economics were largely taught by economics professors with very applied interests in business administration.

As soon as university-based degree programs in business administration began to achieve some degree of legitimacy, both within the university and the society at large, the question of focus emerged. There seemed to be little question that the direction of the nation's business schools should be applied and should serve to meet a specific set of vocational objectives. In those instances where a clean break had been made with economics, and business administration had been allowed to develop on its own, accounting many times became the nucleus of growth for the business school. At New York University, its School of Commerce, Accounts and Finance (1900) was initially charged with the responsibility of preparing students to sit for and pass the state's CPA examinations. The school's first dean was Charles Haskins, a partner in the accounting firm of Haskins and Sells. It should also be noted that the various programs of study at NYU's business school provided for both business skills training (i.e., office practices and teacher training) and careers in public accounting.

The vast majority of the newly formed schools of business administration which developed around the turn of the century had their original ties with departments and faculty in economics. However, many business programs had a more interdisciplinary background which drew upon such fields as political science, public administration as well as other academic subjects. One such program of study was the Wharton School at the University of Pennsylvania (1881). Edmund James, the school's founder, developed a curriculum which focused on government service, history, and economics, along with a much more restricted set of course offerings in the more accepted business subjects such as accounting and business law. In fact it is interesting to note that for the first thirty years of the Wharton School's history, it was housed under the College of Arts and Science and drew heavily on arts and science faculty.

A rich background in liberal arts at the undergraduate level underscored the development of the Harvard Business School. While the faculty committee which established the initial proposal for the school clearly recognised the need for career preparation in business, they were equally convinced that it should follow a more generic undergraduate curriculum. Although the school was initially established in 1908 it was not until 1913 that it was taken from under the administration of the College of Arts and Science and given independent status within the university.

The road to achieving academic legitimacy for business schools across the nation was a difficult one in the years prior to the First World War. Programs at such universities as University of Pennsylvania, Harvard and Chicago, which placed emphasis on practical business skills in specific industrial environments, seemed to have a better probability of success than those programs which maintained their ties to more theoretical economics departments. By the beginning of the First World War the more popular business programs in the east and mid-west offered specific course work leading to careers in such fields as accounting, public service, insurance, banking and secretarial science. It seems clear that the strategy employed by the more accepted business schools focused on clearly defined linkages between degree programs and vocations.

25

As business schools became more vocationally focused, particularly in the last two years of study, they grew both in terms of the number of degrees granted annually as well as with regard to the number of degree programs offered. However, this was less the case with respect to universities and colleges on the west coast of the continent. For example, although an undergraduate program in business had been established at the University of California, Berkeley in 1898, during the pre World War I period, only a very few courses in the field of business were offered. In fact, it was not until the early 1940's that the faculty in business were given independent status within the larger university and were moved from the department of economics.

Finally, during this early period in the collegiate development of business education, it should be noted that the central debate being faced by many schools of business related to the break with traditional and more theoretical academics. Clearly, the popularity and growth of a school of business could be directly related to its practical and vocationally focused curriculum. The closer the linkage between course work and business practice, the greater the probability of success. Alternatively, business schools which had maintained close ties to departments of economics remained considerably less practical in their focus and stressed course work related to such matters as the historical development of business practice, theories of business behavior and government relations.

It seems quite clear that during this pre World War I period, business education in the practical and theoretical university environments lacked in context. There was little in the way of agreements among faculty and administrators as to the central direction business education should take. The precise function of the business organisation in the larger society had not yet been determined to the satisfaction of the academic community, and certainly, without this statement of mission, little could be agreed upon with regard to program development, degree options and specific course work.

THE PRE WORLD WAR II PERIOD

The period between the two World Wars saw the rapid development of business education in the United States. For the most part, public universities were the quickest to respond with private colleges and universities coming on-line with business programs later in this period.

In many instances there was the rapid prolife-ration of degree programs in business administra-tion with little accomplished in the way of buil-ding a solid foundation for such developments. In an effort to keep pace with the needs of industry, and not discourage prospective students, schools of business were organised, business options were developed and courses were taught with the focus on academic expediency and not curriculum integrity. During this period, little existed in regard to instructional support materials such as monographs and texts. More importantly, the professors charged with the responsibility for curriculum development and instruction were themselves many times inadequately prepared.

In 1928, Leon C. Marshall, dean of the Univer-sity of Chicago business school, in a comprehensive report on the state of business education in the US, took a strong position that American business education was sadly lacking. His primary concerns related to the over-development of such programs with inadequate attention directed toward necessary academic rigor and conceptualisation(3).

The rapid expansion of business education in the US during pre-World War II led to several significant outcomes, however. First, almost by virtue of its growth, business education became highly visible both in academic and vocational communities. This visibility was the first step towards its legitimacy at the university and colle-giate level. While academics in the liberal arts and humanities did not quite know what to make of business administration, there was little question that it was here to stay, and ultimately would need to be integrated into higher education in the United States.

Second, although the search process may have seemed to have been unorthodox and random, business administration was taking important initial steps in its development from infancy to adulthood. We must remember that schools of business were among the first professional schools admitted to an academy which had historically placed little value on vocational preparation. For this reason it is not altogether unreasonable that not only would business need to demonstrate its contribution to academia, but additionally, would need to undertake the learning process by which this legitimacy would ultimately emerge.

Third, although it would take many years for a viable plan for business education to evolve in the US, this period prior to World War II had been invaluable, and important accomplishments had been achieved. Specifically, a functional subdivision of business administration had taken place. It was now clear that both the preparation of secondary teachers in business subjects and vocational preparation for careers in business and industry were the output objectives of business schools throughout the nation. Additionally, business vocational degree programs focused on specific industrial arenas. Also, some standardisation had been achieved nationwide with regard to business education. While the years following World War II would see far better refinement with regard to this standardisation issue, the direction had been established that higher education in business schools could not simply develop as the result of local consensus and need.

Fourth, from the beginning, the business community had been involved in the development of business education in the United States. In some instances this could be viewed as a liability in the sense that it may have driven its growth too quickly and not provided the proper time for solid foundation to be built. However, the point still remains that the linkage between American business/ industry and the nation's business schools provided practical direction and vocational education which was relevant and ultimately led to timely and efficient student placement.

THE POST WORLD WAR II PERIOD

In the period immediately preceding World War II, it seemed clear that while business education in the United States had come a long distance since 1900, several important questions would need to be addressed prior to its achievement of full legitimacy. First, there was a critical question relating to the balance between general education and business education. In order for business education to be viewed as more than simply vocational training, particularly by colleagues in other parts of the university, it would need to be preceded by a solid foundation in more general educational subjects. Most business faculty viewed this as a perfectly reasonable position and supported the notion that business students should spend their first two years taking classes in the liberal arts, sciences, humanities, and fine arts. Only after students had successfully completed their general education would business education begin. This general education mandate was to become a standard for the development of collegiate education in business during the post World War II period.

Second, it was abundantly clear that the character of American business was changing. New industries were developing, new technology was being employed and new groups of workers were being linked to new classifications of employment. It would be critical that business education keep pace with the accelerating tempo of business practice. The question still remained however, to what extent should business education actually lead business practice. If it was the responsibility of business education to expeditiously follow and fill the needs created by American commerce and industry then the charge would focus on establishing need and responding with appropriate curriculum. Alternatively, if it was the responsibility of business education to establish the future direction of business practice, applied research would be in order for schools and faculty of business.

Finally, a third important question which would need to be faced early on in the post World War II period related to convergence with regard to precisely what was meant by an education in business administration as preparation for a career in business. Much earlier, general agreement had been reached with respect to what was understood to be the charge of business education for the preparation of secondary school teachers in business subjects. Courses in business skills had been developed to meet this need. However, there was substantially less agreement in regard to a common body of knowledge prerequisite for students desiring careers in banking, insurance, manufacturing and retailing. This would be an area of primary concern as the Second World War ended.

As with most war periods, the Second World War pushed ahead many new frontiers in business and industry. While domestic commercial activity was kept to an absolute minimum through federal laws and regulations, industry directed toward the production of war goods flourished in the United States. Virtually all capable individuals not directly engaged in war combat were put to work in support industries. New manufacturing technology was developed in order to meet the immediate needs of war production, computer and electronic developments supported the logistic and technological problems brought on by the war and new interfaces between people and machines were explored.

There is little question that many of the advancements which we take for granted today in US consumer goods and manufacturing processes had their crude beginnings during the Second World War. Even more importantly, many of the challenges which schools of business in the US have been facing for the past forty years got their early starts during this same period. Matters relating to labor relations, productivity, technological applications and administrative planning and strategy can be quite easily traced back to the conditions of wartime industry in the United States.

The sudden need for the US to become a war production society in 1941, the equally sudden end of the war and the rapid conversion to consumer manufacturing coupled with the emergence of the United States as one of the postwar world powers, left an incredible educational vacuum in the arenas of business and engineering. It would now be the responsibility of the higher educational establishment in the US to gear up to fill this post-World War II educational void.

In the late forties business education in the US flourished. Men returning from Europe and the Pacific could take advantage of the GI Bill, which provided a rich financial incentive to pursue both graduate and undergraduate degree programs. As we mentioned earlier, the conversion from war production to consumer production took record time and, within literally months, US business and industry had geared up to meet the demands of the consumers who had gone without automobiles, household appliances and various other necessities during the war. American business was eager to apply the technology which had been developed during the war in the areas of computers, production methods and electronics. Due to developments such as these, enrollments in schools of business across the nation hit all time highs and predictions for the early fifties looked very optimistic.

Schools of business expanded rapidly during this post World War II period. New specialisations were developed in human relations, marketing, production, operations research and labor relations. American businesses and industry were desperate for graduates with expertise in these areas, were willing to pay well, and offered very desirable career opportunities.

We should also note that during this same period, the demand for secondary teachers in business subjects had substantially increased. The rapid development of the consumer economy in the postwar period had brought with it a need for individuals with skills in bookkeeping, office management, typing, etc. For the most part, these individuals were trained at the high school level or in the private business colleges. In either case, public universities and colleges were needed in order to provide teachers in the business skills areas.

The rapid growth of business education in the late forties and early fifties, that brought prosperity for schools of business, also posed some difficult questions. One of the most critical concerns was related to faculty staffing. Since graduate training in business was itself in its infancy, few individuals existed with the appropriate credentials to teach graduate and undergraduate courses in business subjects. Once again, faculty from other disciplines throughout the university were recruited into schools of business. Professors from economics taught courses in finance, political scientists taught courses in management and forecasting, psychologists added their expertise in human relations and behavior, and · lawyers taught classes in the Uniform Commercial code.

By the early fifties, there began to emerge a set of core concentrations in most business programs throughout the nation. Students were required to take survey courses in accounting, economics, business law, business math, marketing, production methods, corporate finance and management. More focused concentrations existed in secretarial science, insurance, personnel and sales.

THE AMERICAN ASSOCIATION OF COLLEGIATE SCHOOLS OF BUSINESS

Although the American Association of Collegiate Schools of Business (AACSB) was originally founded in 1916 to promote the development of business education in the US, it was really not until the post-World War II period that the association began to exercise a considerable influence over the direction of business education. Dating back to

1926, the AACSB had established a set of program standards which a business school would need to meet prior to being admitted to the association. For example, Standard Nine stated that 'All collegiate schools shall offer a reasonable amount of work in at least five groups of study, such as business finance, accounting, business law, marketing and statistics'(4).

Although the AACSB had a presence in the business education community prior to World War II, it was generally viewed as a forum for the exchange of ideas and not a governing body for the direction of higher education in business. In 1940, some fifty-three schools were members of the AACSB.

By 1958, eighty-five schools had now become members and the impact of the association was considerably stronger. The list of schools seeking membership had grown considerably by this time and the standards for membership specified the nature of the curriculum which should be offered. Specifically, applicant schools should offer instruction in the areas of accounting, economics, statistics, business law, finance, marketing and management.

The rapid development of business education during the early fifties, specifically with regard to masters and doctoral level programs, and the emergence of many new concentrations such as marketing and human relations, left the academic community with major concerns regarding its future course. Somewhat as a response to this general concern, the AACSB sponsored two studies during this period. The Kozelka report (1954) and the Arden House conference on faculty requirements (1956)(5) set the stage for later studies and raised serious concerns regarding the need for more fully developed research in business education and the unification of schools of business across the nation.

The Pierson report(6) and the Gordon and Howell report(7) (both 1959) filled much of the research vacuum created by the earlier AACSB studies. Each of these projects sought to clarify the major issues in business education and establish future directions.

THE EDUCATION OF AMERICAN BUSINESS
(The Pierson Report)

In 1959, Professor Frank C. Pierson of Swarthmore College first published his research findings on

the state of business education in America. This
research was sponsored by the Carnegie Corporation
and was intended to '... assess different
approaches to academic preparation for business
careers'. (Pierson, 1959, pg. ix). While it would
be difficult to suggest that the Pierson findings
revolutionised the direction of business education
in the ensuing years, it did confirm a number of
problem areas.

Professor Pierson's research underscored the
absence of rigor and acceptable standards, particularly at the undergraduate level. He noted that
the societal demands for business graduates had
placed considerable strain on institutions of
higher education. Admission standards, curriculum
requirements, course content, and faculty preparation were all in question. His basic conclusion was
that business education of the period was attempting to accomplish too much and in the process was
losing its integrity and ultimate value to society.

Pierson was particularly concerned with what he
viewed as conflicting charges brought before the
four-year colleges. Not only were these institutions responsible for academic training at the
undergraduate (and in some cases graduate) level,
but additionally,these same institutions shouldered
the burden of teaching business skills, continuing
education in technical subjects and management
development programs. Pierson felt that a substantial portion of the basic level instruction in the
'simpler business skills' should be assumed by the
nation's two-year junior colleges. This would leave
the American business schools to meet a specific
challenge for which they were best qualified.

Pierson continues his research by pointing out
the specific mission of the undergraduate and
graduate business schools of the US. He viewed the
central challenge for these institutions in the
area of applying scientific method and general
societal knowledge to the most significant issues
of business policy. He further maintained that many
business schools throughout the nation were poorly
prepared for this endeavour. Pierson contended
that the vast majority of employers do not require
highly specialised business graduates, but rather,
a curriculum in business administration should
place emphasis on generic business subjects and a
strong background in liberal arts and sciences.

The Pierson report on business education
provided considerable insight into the historical
roots of academic training in business and the

current (as of 1959) state of this particular dimension of higher education. Additionally, through the contributions of various recognised authorities, insightful comments were made with regard to curriculum development. Finally, the Pierson document discusses a variety of less formalised instruction in business administration. For example, management development and evening extension programs.

HIGHER EDUCATION FOR BUSINESS
(The Gordon and Howell Report)

Also in 1959, Robert A. Gordon (University of California, Berkeley) and James E. Howell (Stanford University) published their research findings on the state of higher education in business in the US. This project was funded by the Ford Foundation and took Professors Gordon and Howell three years to complete. Even today the Gordon and Howell report is viewed as one of the most comprehensive studies of university based higher education in business.

The authors of this study recognised the critical role that university based education in business administration would assume in the development and preparation of business leaders of the sixties and seventies. They additionally characterised higher education in business as 'adrift' and in desperate need of goal clarity and direction. Gordon and Howell felt that business schools on university campuses had not established their legitimacy in the academic community and were seeking answers to such fundamental questions as who should teach and what should be taught. They recognised the rapid growth of business education in the preceding decades and saw the problems being that of both quantity and quality of current educational practices. Finally, they saw the responsibility of the Ford Foundation report as not only to provide an overview of the current state of conditions, but additionally, to make recommendations regarding future directions.

In Chapter Two of the study, the authors document the growth of business education in the US. Their findings indicate that in 1919 only 1,576 bachelors' degrees were awarded in business, 110 masters' degrees and no doctors' degrees. However, less than forty years later the respective figures are: 50,090, 5,205 and 109, for the three degree categories. Also in 1919, degrees in business accounted for 3.2 per cent of all degrees awarded in the US. Again, in 1958, this percentage had grown to 12.6.

Not only did the Gordon and Howell report indicate the rapid growth of business education in the US, but additionally, it confirmed the incredible diversity in degree programs and content. Much the same as the Pierson report, these authors viewed this variety in business education as particularly problematic. The following quote from the report summarises their concern.

> Even if we look only at collegiate business education, heterogeneity is still the keynote. Business degrees are confirmed by four-year colleges ranging from converted normal schools to some of the better liberal arts colleges, by technical institutes, and by multipurpose universities. These institutions are public and private, urban and rural, large and small, old and new, good and bad. (Gordon and Howell, 1959, P.25)

In their report, Gordon and Howell viewed the single most important charge of business education to be that of preparation for careers in business and related fields. They further suggest four fundamental elements of business practice which should be addressed in any business curriculum. First, are a set of organisational concerns relating to coordination and administrative relationships. Second, is what they referred to as the 'nonmarket' environment. Such dimensions as political, cultural and social events would be considered here. Third, the 'market' environment relates to economic and commercial activities associated with the production and sale of goods and services. Finally, the fourth ingredient in their business formula related to the economic aspects of business operations. Here, the specifics of procurement, production and sale must be addressed. Professors Gordon and Howell were convinced that before business could truly be viewed as a legitimate profession worthy of academic preparation there would need to be convergence around a set of curricular standards related to these four dimensions of business activity.

Very possibly, the most difficult challenge placed before Professors Gordon and Howell related to the translation of these four dimensions into a mission for higher education in business. They further viewed effective business practice as involving a set of skills. Specifically, 1) skills in recognising, anticipating and solving problems, 2) skills in developing and maintaining effective organisational relationships, and 3) skills in interpersonal relationships and communication.

As mentioned earlier, this research project was certainly one of the most comprehensive studies of higher education in business ever conducted. Its overall evaluation left substantial challenges before the country's business schools. The report left few rocks unturned and was quite specific with regard to what the next steps should be. Higher education in business was chastised for not prac- tising more of what it preached. In short, this meant becoming more focused on environmental demands and more goal directed toward a set of reasonable and logical graduate outcomes.

RECENT DEVELOPMENTS

There seems to be little question that, as during the period of the Ford Foundation report, today higher education in business is under attack. The battle charges are led from forces both within and external to schools and colleges of business. In some instances, the groups which have assembled to debate the future of business education in America have been collections of deans and faculties of business. In other cases, accrediting bodies such as the American Assembly of Collegiate Schools of Business (previously, American Association of Collegiate Schools of Business), have taken to task the charge of business schools, and in still other instances members of the business community, professional associations and university governing bodies have met to review the proper role of business education in the upcoming decades.

The question might be asked, why have so many for so long been so concerned with our country's responsibility for vocational education in business? To a certain degree the answer might be found in the almost overwhelming presence of business education over the past twenty-five years. To date in the US, there are well over 1200 institutions which offer some form of education in business at the post-secondary level. Colleges and universities alone account for over 450 of these programs and currently 240 are accredited by the American Assembly of Collegiate Schools of Business. Twenty-five years ago 13 per cent of all undergraduate degrees in the US (50,000) were granted in business. Today, this percentage has increased to 24 per cent (220,000). The increase has been equally dramatic at the masters level. In 1963, six per cent of all graduate degrees were in business, and in recent years this figure has approached as high as ten per cent.

This rapid growth of higher education in business has not been without cost. Recently, respected authors and the popular press have taken business schools to task. They have been charged with inflating the value of their graduates, particularly at the most prestigious MBA granting institutions. The chronic productivity problem of the US manufacturing sector has also been placed on the collective shoulders of our business schools and Tom Peters (co-author of In Search of Excellence) was recently quoted as having said that 'the business schools... are doing more harm than good'. Regardless of the severity of the problems facing our country's schools of business, rapid and radical change in institutions of higher education is a scarce commodity. Just as with the recommendations of the Ford Foundation and Carnegie Corporation reports, it will take time for academia to digest the issues and charge itself with new direction. However, it would appear as though the time is appropriate for making recommendation and schools of business throughout the nation may be willing to listen. Recent events with regard to the ethical behavior of corporate America, international matters of trade deficits and the continuous erosion of the US manufacturing/industrial sector cannot be ignored, and it is clear that higher education in business may be part of both the problem as well as the solution. In the following paragraphs of this section we will discuss a number of the issues facing today's schools of business in the US.

The Lessons which are still with us from the Ford Foundation Report

Although we are now approaching thirty years since the publication of the Ford Foundation Report, many of the concerns Professors Gordon and Howell left with us still exist. These researchers were convinced that the best preparation for a career in business should begin with undergraduate training in the liberal arts followed by an MBA. With this recommendation in mind, they further suggested that there was far too much emphasis placed on under-graduate business education at the sacrifice of graduate level research and program development. Today in the US undergraduate training in business still dominates the academic scene and severely limits the resources allocated to masters and doctoral level funding.

A second issue raised by the Gordon and Howell report, which remains today, relates to the application of the computer to business education. In 1959, the authors of the Ford Foundation Report viewed the 'computer revolution' as on the horizon for business education. At this time they were uncertain as to what its implications would be and how it should be integrated into business activities. Today, there is little question that computers are a vital component of the main stream of business activity, yet there are still important questions to be answered regarding their proper role in undergraduate and graduate business education. As the function of management becomes more time sensitive and demanding and computers reach higher capabilities and approach intelligent systems, will the function of the computer be supportive or destructive? In other words, will the computer have the capacity of making certain managerial functions redundant and should this be a logical extension of computer technology? Although many of the initial concerns of the Gordon and Howell Report regarding computerisation may have passed, the computer still remains an important issue to be addressed in today's business schools.

The Gordon and Howell Report also addressed the issues of needless specialisation in business schools. They understood full well how prolifera-tion of degree options in business served the needs of administrators and professors, however, they were equally convinced that it did little to meet market requirements. Today, in business schools the emphasis on specialisation continues and degree concentrations in such areas as international business, management information systems, strategic planning, and business ethics abound. In 1988, as in 1959, there is little attempt to question the need for such specialisation.

A fourth issue raised by the Ford Foundation study related to the general architecture of the university and the proper placement of professional schools in general, and business schools in particular. The growth of business education (along with computer science and engineering) has drained scarce resources from other parts of the campus. The question which has presented itself in recent years relates to the point at which a university must resist the student demand forces which will turn it toward professional training at the risk of sacrificing its larger mission of higher education. (4)

This same problem also exists at the micro level within business schools. Over the past several decades, certain majors, for example management and production, have lost enrollments while others have grown. This has resulted in the redistribution of internal resources toward those programs which have the highest student demand. So, we can easily see that this same architectural integrity question must be addressed by school planning committees and deans. To the extent that it is not, we will continue to see the erosion of generalist training in favor of even greater specialisation.

A final point raised by the Ford Foundation Report, which is clearly an important issue today, relates to environmental change. Although in 1959 Professors Gordon and Howell viewed the problem of highly dynamic business environments and their effective management as secondary, today this would hardly be the case. Over the past decades such environmental forces as increased foreign competition, maturing production technology, equal employment opportunity, and population demographics have placed severe demands on American businesses. Only recently have business schools responded with course work, text materials, and teaching models which incorporate the analysis and management of complex economic and social environments.

From the above discussion we should be able to recognise that while the 1959 Ford Foundation Report on higher education in business set the stage for important changes in the ensuing decades, in some instances it has not been enough. In the following paragraphs of this section we will address some of the issues which have arisen for business education in the period between the Gordon and Howell Report and the present.

Management Education in the United States

Macro Level Issues

At the most macro level there appears to be a set of issues which surround the activities of the university-based business school. These are products of recent environmental shifts and will need to be addressed by administrators and faculty of today's and tomorrow's schools of business. The following list is by no means exhaustive, but rather, this author's perception of the most pressing of these problems.

Integration with Non-business Fields
Today in the US, institutional areas which were at one time considered far removed from 'business' are finding themselves being mainstreamed into business values and practices. In some instances, these fields of endeavor are climbing on the business bus willingly and in other cases are being forced.

Traditionally, non-business vocational arenas such as health care, science, recreation, municipal governance and education are finding it absolutely necessary to give recognition to the business and commercial aspects of their operations today in the US. They are recognising considerable success in applying business promotional concepts in order to increase their market share in more competitive customer environments and they are seeing the need to plan more effectively through budgeting and various business accounting principles.

In order for these new members of the business community to become more fully integrated into US commercial practices, it will be necessary for schools of business to adapt. Programs and course work will need to direct attention to their unique concerns in the world of business and yet provide these new ventures with practical business wisdom. Today, we see joint ventures between colleges of medicine and business in producing graduate students in health care administration. Also, undergraduate students in recreation take required courses in business in order to find vocational placement in municipal parks and recreation departments. This is only the beginning of new organisations and classifications of employment designed to bring the world of business into the non-business institutions of the 21st century.

Market Share Competition
It has been estimated that between 40 and 45 billion dollars will be spent in 1988 on business

40

education in the US. This number included all forms of business-related training both on and off university campuses. However, it should also be recognised that only a small fraction of this total amount, possibly 12 to 15 per cent, will cover the expense of graduate and undergraduate training in business.

The above numbers suggest that business related education in the US is truly a huge industry and it is additionally worthy to note that the trend has been in favor of non-university based programs. This growth has not gone unnoticed by business school deans and faculty and has sponsored significant attempts to capture these lucrative markets. Continuing education, executive development and short technical courses are found today in most urban universities. However, the competition from professional associations, union organisations, and private institutions and corporations is intense and schools of business must be given poor marks with regard to their ability to focus on this professional market's needs.

The extent that this decline in market-share for schools of business represents a significant problem may be debatable. Some would contend that meeting these market needs actually detracts from the mission of higher education while others would point out the need to serve both community and student interests. Regardless of its rightness or wrongness, the fact remains that our nation's schools of business are finding a less prominent position in the education of their professional constituencies. It is difficult to speculate as to the future of this issue. However, it will certainly be a matter of discussion for schools of business, accrediting bodies and professional organisations in the years to come.

Environmental Uncertainty

Today we have accepted as an article of faith that the conditions that business must face are increasingly uncertain. It would seem as though the era of predictable times met a sudden death with the OPEC cartel in the early 1970s. It has been from this point until today that we have seen new industries and businesses take hold over night, and others abruptly vanish. In the US we have entire industries with long histories of regulation freed from government support to prosper or fail on their own and we have witnessed the need for this same government to intervene in our sacred free market system to breathe new life into dying industrial giants.

It seems clear that the business graduates of today and tomorrow will need to withstand sudden death blows to their organisations and, at the same time, capture the moment for immediate opportunity. Today in schools of business throughout the US, centers and course work in entrepreneurship, creativity, and innovation have found their place and students seem eager to integrate these ideas with more traditional business wisdom.

Although this author is not completely convinced that the vast majority of business schools which expound on the virtues of innovation and creativity have the capacity to translate these concepts into meaningful theory, practice, and course work for students, there does appear to be a common message. It is that the concept of planning, which has worked so well for business and industry for the past thirty years, was based on the continuation of trends. Today, we are part of an era of abrupt shifts which have the capacity to reconstitute entire industries next door and around the world. Graduates in business must be prepared to either anticipate these changes, and quickly adjust, or fail.

The Relevancy of Research

For the past thirty years, schools of business in the US have been to a large degree stockpiling the efforts of faculty research. An incredibly small portion of this effort ever finds its way into the actual practice of business. Faculty publish their findings in scholarly journals of which the readership is almost entirely other professors within their specific discipline. Additionally, these same faculty present the findings of their scientific inquiry at regional and national professional meetings, which are almost never attended by practicing business men and women.

It would seem to this author that the time is appropriate for the rich rewards of this three plus decades of research to be tested and evaluated in the most relevant community—the practicing world of business. To some extent recent attempts have been made to incorporate business practitioners into an arena of university-based research. The recent addition of the Academy of Management Executive to the journal list of the Academy of Management is surely a welcome addition in this regard and, of course, some journals and professional associations have longer histories directed toward the application of research findings. Any attempt in this direction should be encouraged and promoted by business schools in the coming decades.

Internationalisation of American Business Education

In the 1984-85 Standards and Guidelines for business school accreditation, offered by the AACSB it states: 'Every student should be exposed to the international dimension through one or more elements of the curriculum'. While the AACSB is quite clear as to the necessity for international exposure it is equally unclear as to how this objective should be accomplished. Should a school or college of business desiring to maintain or achieve accreditation add specific courses in international finance, marketing and management or should the international dimension be integrated into existing common body of knowledge requirements?

Although matters of implementation are being seriously debated today, the necessity to 'internationalise' is not. The basic problem curriculum committees, departments, and individual faculty face is that we do not know how to meet the spirit of the AACSB standard. The United States was incredibly late in becoming a member of the world economic community and both its businesses and its business education sadly reflect it. We are learning today, through AACSB workshops and professional meetings, how to conquer the international problem and the cross-cultural business literature is finding its way into textbooks, courses and specific concentration.

It is also clear that we have not done nearly enough with regard to preparing our students for careers in world economics and management practices. Today, many undergraduate programs have chosen to add elective courses in international business, however, these programs may not require such course work for graduation. This becomes an even greater problem at the MBA level where fewer electives are required and offered.

A second component of the international problem relates to faculty preparation. Although many schools of business in the US are finding that appointments of foreign faculty, both on a temporary and permanent basis, enrich the international offerings, indigenous faculty are often quite unprepared to integrate matters of foreign significance into their courses.

The American business school stands quite alone in the world community with respect to this problem. Her sister institutions in Western Europe, Australia, or throughout Asia have recognised their dependency as a part of a world community for decades.

Today, US schools of business are looking to the rest of the world for instruction on this matter. We need assistance with regard to curricula design, course content and faculty development. We are attempting to attract faculty with teaching interests in the international arena as well as encouraging current faculty to take leaves of absence overseas. The international issue will become increasingly important to US business education and we will continue to need help in achieving its full integration into our schools and colleges of business.

The AACSB

Today, the AACSB continues to be a significant force in the relevant environment of many schools and colleges of business through the US. This association, through its published standards, establishes the direction higher education in business should pursue for two classifications of degree programs. First, those institutions which currently are fully accredited by the AACSB must, through a self-generated report, sit for a reaccreditation review every five years. Additionally, every ten years a self-study must be followed by a site visitation by representatives of the AACSB. Second, those institutions which are seeking accreditation by the AACSB must constantly build their academic program(s) toward the guidelines of this accrediting body.

With regard to acquiring accreditation or reaccreditation, the AACSB is concerned with virtually all aspects of an institution's degree program(s) in business. Some of the issues which are of highest concern are: curriculum and course content, faculty qualifications, research productivity of faculty, library and computer facilities, student admission and graduation standards, faculty utilisation and course coverage and instructional methods. As it currently stands, the AACSB will accredit both bachelors and masters level programs, however, no attempt has been made to provide this same service at the Ph.D. or DBA level.

For those schools and colleges of business which are currently accredit or seeking accredita-

tion in the near future, there is little question
that the AACSB directs a considerable amount of the
decision-making associated with the education
process. As shifts in emphasis occur in the
standards of the accrediting body (for example, in
recent years the AACSB has placed additional
emphasis on the international and ethical aspects
of business education) member schools must also
modify their courses and curricula.

The AACSB also provides substantial support to
member schools through its regional and national
meetings as well as workshops for faculty and
administrators. Through these programs, the AACSB
is continually keeping member schools updated on
future changes in governing standards and assisting
them in meeting these objectives.

Micro Level Issues

So far in this section we have only addressed those
issues facing schools and colleges of business
which have their origin in the institution's
environment. Additionally, there is a set of
events which are more local to the institution. We
will discuss several of these concerns below.

Increased Specialisation
As we have already mentioned, almost thirty years
ago Professors Gordon and Howell alerted the
readers of their report as to what they considered
to be the excessive level of specialisation in
their sample schools. The issue of specialisation
in today's business schools is far from dead.
Rather, specialisation, and possibly in some
instance overspecialisation, tend to be the norm
and general standard by which schools grow and
develop.

Specialisation is in every sense a double-edged
sword. From one perspective, in order for a school
of business to meet both faculty expectations and
technological developments, specialisation must
occur. As business systems become increasingly more
complex and demanding general business training
will need to give way to functional and hierarchical refinement. Alternatively, however, higher and
higher degrees of specialisation require improved
generalist training in order to bring to bear the
necessary forces of integration and coordination.

Today, many colleges of business have developed
highly specialised programs in accounting and have

even spun-off somewhat independent schools of accountancy within the larger colleges of business. To support this endeavor, the AACSB has recently provided for separate accreditation procedures and standards for schools of accountancy. Should this trend continue, we may witness the eventual disintegration of schools of business into even greater sub-specialties than we find them today. This is not unlike other professional schools such as medicine, engineering, and law, where, in order to meet the academic demands of their respective disciplines, cohesion and solidarity have given way to independence and competition.

Integration

The flip side of the specialisation issue relates to the need to integrate or reintegrate. Once again, the Ford Foundation Report provides us with some historic commentary on this matter. Professors Gordon and Howell in 1959 suggested a model for the future development of business degree programs organised around three generic disciplines: economics, behavioral science, and applied mathematics. These academic fields would serve as the research and literature foundation for any school of business and the various functional subdivisions of the business school (finance, management, marketing... etc.) would draw on the intellectual wisdom of the generic disciplines. In this way the functional divisions of any school of business would maintain a general business integrity based on the three common properties of their model.

Over the years, various schools have flirted with variations of the Gordon and Howell model. In the 1950s, programs at Carnegie Mellon University and the University of Chicago attempted to link their curricula to foundations in economics, mathematics and human behavior. More recently, several graduate programs on campuses of the University of California have attempted to create interdisciplinary schools of management or administration. Here the model has been to integrate the academic disciplines of business and public administration. In order to achieve this objective, faculty have been hired with academic backgrounds and research interests in political science, economics, sociology, psychology, and business. The challenges of building curricula and making strategic decisions within this type of interdisciplinary environment are obvious and, in many cases, these programs turn out to be more multidisciplinary than they are interdisciplinary. Regardless of their success or form, schools of business will continue to face the responsibility of integrating increasingly diverse sets of degree programs and faculty resources.

Growth Management
In one sense, schools of business across the United States have practiced exactly what they have been preaching. Over the past two decades, the demand for business graduates has been unprecedented and our universities have responded to market demand with dramatic growth. In many instances this growth has allowed schools and colleges of business to become the largest academic unit on our respective campuses.

There is a perspective, however, which suggests that all this growth is actually counterproductive. Supporters here would maintain that a more regulated growth is far more advisable and would help to guarantee a higher quality educational process as well as a far superior business graduate. They would continue by suggesting that we accomplish little by turning out large numbers of marginal students who achieve minimal career success and do little to strengthen the reputations of our nation's schools of business.

Growth can be highly seductive to any organisation. To a school of business it may appear to bring with it legitimacy, resources and recognition. Alternatively, growth which is not correctly directed toward rational and reasonable objectives may actually serve to erode the administrative process. At a certain point, each school of business must be willing to evaluate the necessity for further growth and, very possibly, decide that additional students, facilities, and faculty may create more harm than good.

Business Education in a Post-Industrial Society
Recent authors in the US popular press, for example, Naisbitt(8), April 12, 1988, Toffler(9), Drucker(10) have presented a convincing argument that, for the past several years, we have been embarking on a post-industrial era. Many of us in the United States are unwilling to accept the notion that our industrial society will need to give way to an information and knowledge society.

Our country grew to a great world position largely because we could build things better and cheaper than any other country in the world. This is certainly no longer the case. Rather, we find

that many other countries around the world are
quite capable of out-producing our manufacturing
sector. Our recent history of a monumental trade
deficit provides us with ample proof of this
contention.

Schools of business grew to maturity in our
country during the industrial era and now have to
face highly uncertain times. Today's business
school graduates no longer seek employment opportunities in the manufacturing sector, but rather,
pursue careers in industries and businesses which
sell information, knowledge, and high-tech
services. These modern industrial environments
change abruptly with little warning and allow only
a limited amount of time for people and businesses
to catch up.

Schools of business in the US today are having
to experiment and learn quickly. It seems all too
clear that many of the business standards which
worked so well in the past will only have limited
success in our future. Today's graduates will be
facing new markets with products and services which
presently do not exist. They will be applying new
technologies to problems and opportunities we have
little knowledge of and will be managing people
with different values and preparation in jobs which
today do not exist.

Much the same as the challenges our country
faced almost one hundred years ago when it quickly
shifted from a rural farming society into an industrialised nation, once again we are charged with a
monumental responsibility. If America is to survive
as a world leader it will only do so through the
resource of its people. Many of these people will
need to be developed and trained for the work of
the 21st century in the business schools of today.
There are some who might suggest that the highly
dynamic characteristics of this type of post-
industrial environment will make a college or
university education in business obsolete and
irrelevant. Others might be a little more optimistic in their predictions and recommend that a more
general education in business administration is
more appropriate under these dynamic circumstances.
This would be opposed to an approach which places
emphasis on methods and techniques which all have
the capacity to become outdated overnight. In
either instance the future of higher education in
business administration must be approached with
some degree of risk and tentativeness.

Business Ethics

Recent developments in the United States have brought considerable attention to the issue of business ethics. Insider trading on the New York Stock Exchange, the less than ethical/legal practices of US businesses operating in foreign countries, and overtly illegal behavior of executives in Fortune 1000 corporations have all convinced the American public that US business should not be allowed to establish a separate set of ethical and legal standards which are inconsistent with acceptable social norms of conduct.

Largely through public pressure and accrediting requirements, schools and colleges of business across the US have recently made significant attempts to integrate issues relating to business ethics into course materials. Here the issue is that men and women should not be allowed exemption from ordinary rules of social practice simply by virtue of the position they hold in business and industry. Rather, in many instances due to the nature of the business and the position of the person in question, men and women in business may be accountable to higher standards of ethical behavior than other members of society.

In some instances, schools of business have added to their curriculum required courses in business ethics. These courses may challenge students, through case examples, to assume a particular position and respond to a difficult ethical or legal problem facing a business. This problem may make it absolutely necessary for management to forego profits in favor of a more socially appropriate strategic objective. In the case of a single course in business ethics, the entire semester may be devoted to the analysis and discussion of a variety of ethical and legal problems.

In the majority of instances, however, issues relating to ethical business practices have been integrated into existing courses. The courses which lend themselves most readily to the presentation of ethical issues are courses in business, government and society, courses in business law and the 'capstone' or strategy and policy course. In many schools and colleges of business throughout the US, it is expected that the professor will consciously bring matters of business ethics into the course content of one or more of these required courses.

Much the same as the issue of international business, today's business schools in America are still experimenting with the matter of business

ethics. While we recognise its importance in a
curriculum in business administration it is not at
all clear nor a matter of substantial agreement as
to how it should be integrated into courses and
curricula.

CONCLUSIONS

In the previous paragraphs we have discussed the
growth and development of higher education in
business administration in the United States. We
have also taken particular note of the criticisms
which have been brought against our business
educational system and have examined some of the
challenges which will need to be faced in the
upcoming years. At this point we will turn our
attention to a set of recommendations which might
serve as general guidelines for the restructuring
of business education on college and university
campuses in the upcoming years.

It would certainly be overly presumptuous to
suggest that what is to follow is anything more
than this author's modest observations as the
result of more than twenty years as a student of
business practices and education in the United
States.

To this author it seems as though business
schools across the United States will need to face
three major generic challenges in the upcoming
decades: 1) the relevancy of their research and
teaching; 2) to whom or what they will be
accountable; and 3) the modification of very
conservative educational practices. In the
following paragraphs we will briefly comment on
each of these challenges/objectives.

Relevancy
For the past seventy or eighty years business
education and research in business in the US has
focused on an ever-increasing number of techniques
and methods. Open any introductory or advanced
textbook in accounting, finance, production, or
computer application and you will find techniques
for capital budgeting, inventory control, effective
cash management or optimising production decisions.
We are certainly not suggesting that a solid foundation in the various methods of business is not
important. Today, in an environment filled with
increased competition and strategies for retrenchment they are probably more critical than ever.

However, today's dynamic and hostile business environments demand more than basic training in methods and techniques. Today's business students must be prepared for continued self-education which places emphasis on seizing the learning opportunities from each new experience.

Recent authors (Raymond, 1986(11), Peters and Waterman, 1982(12)) have commented on the almost formula nature of business conditions, business research, and business education over the past forty years. These same authors have suggested that the business decision-makers of tomorrow's organisations will need to develop new models on their own and make very critical decisions regarding when and how to apply these models to the problems and opportunities they will surely face.

The above suggested scenario places a quite different challenge in front of higher education in business. We must develop in our students an understanding and appreciation for relevant and highly situational information, models for analysis, synthesis and deductive reasoning as well as a willingness to take risks in an entrepreneurial and creative way.

It should be obvious that we are not suggesting minor fine-tuning or the micro-modification of current educational practices. Rather, what is being proposed is substantial reform in a highly traditional and conservative institutional system. This is an issue we will address further in later paragraphs of this section.

Much the same as our educational content, our research in business administration has been equally technique-focused. Highly respected researchers in such diverse functional areas as information systems, managerial finance and organisational behavior have developed their reputations through empirical studies which test the adequacy of computer programs, portfolio selection models and theories of worker satisfaction. In far too many instances both the original research questions as well as the findings of these scientific investigations have either been irrelevant to the business community or have gone unnoticed. Surely the time has come to assure true relevancy with respect to research in business.

What is required in order for business research to better serve the needs of both the business community and the university student seems all too obvious. First, there must be dialogue and meeting of the minds between our business leaders and those of us involved in advancing knowledge with regard to business behavior. Second, adequate rewards must exist in academia for research which serves the needs of the business community and not simply of interest to other academics. Finally, an emphasis on empirical and data-based research may need to give way to valuable and insightful wisdom-based contributions.

Accountability

American schools of business serve many constituencies. Accrediting bodies, students, faculty, business advisory boards and the universities of which they are a part all have interests in the decisions and actions of the schools of business. It goes without saying that only on rare occasions do the agendas of these various interest groups complement each other and, thus, provide the school of business in question with clear and agreed upon guidelines for future direction.

The accommodation which has been made by many schools of business in the US has been largely to ignore those constituencies which would most easily allow it and direct their attention to those groups which would least tolerate neglect. As we have already mentioned, in too many instances this has resulted in a deaf ear being turned to the needs of the business community. Alternatively, the wishes of accrediting bodies (such as the AACSB) and faculty normally cannot be ignored and these groups seem to have played a rather pivotal role in the development of business education across the US.

It is not the intention of this discussion to suggest that any particular constituency group is any more or less important than another. Rather, it is this author's position that US schools of business have created a specific model of higher education in business largely as a result of what they have been willing to consider and what has gone unnoticed or ignored. It seems quite apparent that if schools and colleges of business across our nation are going to grow and develop in an effective and productive manner, new constituencies will need to be considered.

It is most difficult to even begin to suggest who or what these constituencies will represent. The possibilities today, as we look toward the beginning of the twenty-first century, are infinite. However, one thing as Americans we must recognise, is that, in a number of very important ways, we are a unique society by world standards.

The social model of our early development consciously set out to provide for a separation between
our social institutions. In this tradition, we have
gone to great extremes to provide impregnable
boundaries between government, industry, religion,
education, labor..etc. In other societies of the
world, due to necessity or the existence of an
alternative model, this level of specialisation and
separation does not exist. Very possibly, as we
move more and more toward a world economic/
commercial community, our social barriers will seem
less and less appropriate.

If the above scenario is a realistic one it
will bring with it opportunities as well as problems. Support and trust among social institutions
will be critical and independence and autonomous
behavior will be sacrificed. Very possibly, US
higher education in business will be called on to
play a pivotal role in this transition or, alternatively, may be left behind continuing to address
the issue of: to whom are we accountable?

Adaptability
It is difficult, if not impossible, to argue with
the notion that social institutions such as higher
education need to adapt. The real and fundamental
questions relate to the direction, level and
process for change.

In our business schools we have consciously
built-in mechanisms for the modification of
curricula, coursework, graduation standards... etc.
Recruitment of new faculty, policies against in-
breeding, accreditation standards and business
advisory councils are but a few methods by which we
attempt to guarantee an academic program which is
routinely up for review and designed to meet the
needs of our society. However, even with these
mechanisms in place, there is good reason to
believe that we are not doing enough. As business
and industry conditions have become increasingly
complex and time-frames more compact, business
schools have found it more and more difficult to
keep pace with social expectations. New majors or
concentrations must be developed overnight, new
faculty must be recruited, new courses designed
and, above all, academic standards must not be
compromised. This is clearly best exemplified by
today's business concentrations in Management
Information Systems, where technological change
causes hardware, software and course content to
become obsolete overnight.

Governance and planning models for American higher education were never designed with expediency and responsiveness in mind. Our standards of operation, norms of behavior and organisational structure attempt to maximise faculty-participation, collegiality and bureaucratic behavior. It is not altogether certain that such a model will continue to serve the needs of business education and research in the coming decades.

As certain as this author is with regard to the above-mentioned need for adaptation and change and the nature of academic governance, he is equally convinced that an alternative model with a quicker response-time is not likely to arise in the near future. Business schools across the US have long and glorious histories of conservative practices and faculty and administrators have vested interests in the maintenance of past behaviors. One scenario suggests that we may become victims of our pasts, however successful they may have been.

However, there is an alternative. The current popular press in America is replete with examples of businesses which took risks, did things differently and were willing to live with their successes and failures. Innovation, adaptation and change may not come in organised, purposeful and systematic procedures. Rather, they may need spontaneity and immediate action. In the classroom we challenge students to be creative, capture a flash of genius and take calculated risks. Possibly the time has come for us to incorporate these same standards and expectations into our own behaviors.

Finally, it is the hope of this author that this chapter has provided the reader with some new information, some questions regarding the future direction of higher education in business and, most importantly, some food for thought.

NOTES

1. L.V. Douglas, Business Education, Center for Applied Research, Washington, D.C. (1963).
2. National Educational Association, 100 Years in Business Education, NEA, Washington D.C. (1982).
3. L.C. Marshall, (ed), The Collegiate School of Business, University of Chicago Press, Chicago, Ill (1928).
4. R.L. Kozelka, Professional Education for Business, American Association of Collegiate Schools of Business, Minneapolis (1954).
5. Arden House, Faculty Requirements and Standards in Collegiate Schools of Business, American Association of Collegiate Schools of Business, New York (1956).
6. F.C. Pierson, The Education of American Business: A Study of University-College Programs in Business Administration, McGraw-Hill, New York (1959).
7. R.A. Gordon, and J.E. Howell, Higher Education in Business, Columbia University Press, New York (1959).
8. J. Naisbitt, Megatrends, Bantam Books, New York (1982).
9. A. Toffler, The Third Wave, Scott, Foresman and Company, Glenview, Ill (1986).
10. P.F. Drucker, Innovation and Entrepreneurship: Practice and Principles, Harper and Row, New York (1985).
11. A.H. Raymond, Management in the Third Wave, Scott, Foresman and Company, Glenview, Ill (1986).
12. T.J. Peters and R.H. Waterman, In Search of Excellence, Harper and Row, New York (1982).

Chapter Three

MANAGEMENT EDUCATION IN GREAT BRITAIN
Bernard Barry

Although Britain was in the van of the Industrial
Revolution and has been a major industrial nation
for two hundred years, social attitudes towards
industry have been less favourable than in many
other advanced industrial nations. The general
mores of British society have favoured the amateur
tradition and nowhere can this be more clearly
discerned than in industry and commerce where
managers have tended to rely far more on pragmatism
than on formal training. Although there are some
signs of change, managers in Britain are accorded
less status and prestige than those in more traditional professions and are less well-regarded than
their counterparts overseas. Until comparatively
recently, this lack of social recognition had
resulted in careers in management being perceived
as less attractive than those in other fields and
little provision was made to prepare people for
careers in management. Although considerable
developments in the field of management education
have taken place - particularly during the last
twenty-five years - two major reports published in
1987 have shown that the investment made in managerial skills in Britain lags far behind that in
France, West Germany, the United States and Japan.
The first report by John Constable and Roger
McCormick(1) was prepared for the British Institute
of Management and the Confederation of British
Industry. The second report - sponsored by the
Manpower Services Commission, the National Economic
Development Office and the British Institute of
Management - was by Charles Handy.(2)

And
rewards!

56

The reports demonstrate that compared with their counterparts in other advanced nations, British managers are under-educated and poorly trained. They show that only 21 per cent of all British managers hold degrees or professional qualifications and less than a quarter of senior managers in Britain hold degrees compared with 85 per cent in Japan and the United States. In addition to a first degree, many American managers also hold law degrees and 54 per cent of the directors on the supervisory boards of West Germany's 100 largest companies have doctorates either in law or in disciplines such as engineering or science. This paucity of tertiary education amongst British managers, compared with their foreign counterparts, is compounded by the fact that university education in Britain tends to be of a shorter duration and more specialised than in other countries. In West Germany, for example, first degree programs are longer (they range from 4-7 years) and include subjects such as business economics which provide students with an introduction to some basic business skills. The reports show that, not only are British managers less well prepared for their careers before they begin work, but also that relatively little is done to train them at the post-experience stage. The BIM/CBI Report suggests that the average manager in Britain receives the equivalent of one day's formal training each year and more than a third of all middle managers had received no training whatsoever. The Handy Report showed that, in 1986, 21 per cent of companies with over 1000 employees made no provision at all for management training and the figure reached 75 per cent in smaller companies. It also revealed that, even in the larger companies where management training did take place, less than half the managers in these organisations took part in such activity. Handy reports that in the USA, on the other hand, 42 per cent of the top 500 companies provide more than five days off-the-job training per year to each manager. The average British company spends only about 0.14 per cent of turnover on all employee training: a level of funding which suggests that this activity is accorded little importance or recognition by most senior managers. Succession plans, it is reported, are rare. As in recent years there has been a resurgence in the competitiveness of British industry and a growing realisation of the critical role of management in improving the performance of organisations, such findings have generated a great deal of interest and some concern amongst those in industry, government and the academic world. In many ways, therefore, British management education at the present time may be seen to be poised for change.

THE BACKGROUND

The genesis of management education and training in Britain is not easy to discern and there has always been a number of routes to management posts. Some individuals have reached management roles on promotion from the shop floor, relying on instinct and learning from their experiences. Family businesses have always invested in the development of family members destined to hold senior posts in their organisations and have provided varied training for such family heirs. In the period between the two world wars a small number of companies (e.g. ICI, Shell and Unilever) ran internal courses for their managers, but little was offered by the universities and colleges to those preparing themselves for a career in management. Notable exceptions were the Manchester College of Science and Technology (now part of the University of Manchester) and the London School of Economics and Political Science, which both offered a full-time postgraduate course in the 1930's. In addition, a number of universities (e.g. Birmingham, Edinburgh and Liverpool) offered Bachelor of Commerce degree programs and industrial administration courses for students taking engineering degrees, but these were mainly theoretical in orientation and intended to cover a much wider field than careers in management. As there was no obvious route to a career in management, it is not surprising that, in a nation where professional qualifications were highly regarded large numbers of people prepared themselves for a managerial career by undertaking training in accountancy. To this day, 10 per cent of British undergraduates at university intend to serve articles in accountancy. This well-established route, therefore, with many accountants moving into managerial careers, is still very popular. This is reflected in the fact that Britain currently has 120,000 accountants, about 20 times as many as Japan and some 30 times more than West Germany. Apart from bodies serving the accountancy profession, other professional and accrediting institutions have also flourished in Britain. It is assumed that this occurred because of the lack of interest shown by the universities in vocational training and such bodies developed to fill this gap. Britain still does not have technical or vocational institutions similar to the grandes {coles in France, the Technische Hochschulen in West Germany or the Massachusetts Institute of Technology in the United States. (The closest British equivalent of such schools would be the writer's own institution - the Cranfield Institute of Technology. This university-level institution, established in 1946, is the largest centre for applied research, development and design for industry in Western Europe, and specialises in advanced teaching and applied research in engineering, management, public policy and technology).

A number of developments took place in the period between 1946 and 1960 which combined to bring about a reduction in the hostility shown by businessmen to the concept of formal training in management. Some people had been impressed by the results achieved as a result of officer training in the Services during World War II. There was a growing interest in raising productivity by adopting American management methods which people had observed during the War. Finally, as a result of the 1944 Education Act, there was an increase in the number of university graduates and many of these, together with a large number of ex-servicemen, were interested in careers in business. Despite this change in the intellectual climate, in his 1947 report 'Education for Management'(3), (the first report recommending a national system of management education), Colonel Urwick, thought it appropriate to point out: 'There is no implication in this report that young men or women can be trained as managers in industry or commerce by following certain courses of study'. More and more companies began to recruit graduates as management trainees and, as these individuals became more senior in their organisations, the attitudes of at least some senior managers to management education became more favourable. During most of this period, the bulk of management training was provided by the technical colleges. In 1956, a report listing 188 management courses in the United Kingdom showed that two-thirds of these were offered by such colleges. The British Institute of Management was founded in 1947 and launched its Diploma of Management Studies (obtained after completion of a part-time course at a college) in 1949. By 1960, 60 colleges were offering courses leading to this qualification and 1000 students were enrolled in such programs. In the light of other developments taking place,it was decided to re-appraise the Diploma scheme in 1960 and the then Ministry of Education and the British Institute of Management introduced a new and more demanding course. This required part-time study for a period of at least three years, a minimum entry age of 23 and the possession of a degree or appropriate professional qualification. The scheme was also revised in 1964 when the British Institute of Management gave up the administration of the scheme which was taken over by the Department of Education and Science and, at a later stage, by the Council for National Academic Awards. Some seventy institutions now provide courses with an annual average output of 25 per institution. During the period 1977-85 the output of these diploma courses at polytechnics and colleges was approximately 1800 per year. Although there has been some recent growth in the number of enrolments, these have yet to be reflected in the output figures.

Apart from the developments taking place in the technical colleges and the number of companies setting up their own internal management centres, a number of independent management centres were established. The best known of these is the Administrative Staff College (now known as Henley: The Management College) which was set up at Henley-on-Thames in 1946. This institution arose from an initiative by a group of people with experience in industry, commerce and the public service and, with support from the Nuffield Trust, was financed by fees charged to students and subscriptions from industry, commerce and the public sector. Subsequently, Henley provided a model for a large number of sister colleges to be found throughout the world. Another major independent centre - Ashridge Management College - was formed by a group of businessmen in 1959. Other centres, such as Ashorne Hill and Woking, were also set up by companies during this time. Such colleges provided short non-award courses for experienced managers and, when seeking people for such programs, looked not for academic qualifications but practical experience. It is of interest and significance that these trend-setting institutions of their time were established outside the formal educational system and owed their existence largely to the initiative and support of groups of practising managers. Although such colleges have played an important role in establishing residential management education in Britain and, in most cases, have continued to expand, they could not meet more than a small fraction of the needs of the nation for management training. It was in recognition of this that the Foundation for Management Education was set up in 1960 by a group of industrialists and politicians determined to encourage British universities to recognise management as a field of intellectual endeavour and thus - hopefully - contribute to the solution of some of the nation's economic and industrial problems.

During the 1950's, some interest in management education was aroused in the universities. Seven universities introduced one year full-time post-graduate courses and thirteen developed a range of short courses some of which were residential. Industry and commerce appeared ambivalent to these initiatives. Although the residential programs for experienced managers were over-subscribed, few organisations recognised the value of postgraduate programs. Many of those in industry and commerce were suspicious of these innovations and sceptical about the relevance of what university teachers could offer managers or potential managers. Universities were perceived by many senior managers as being too academic and inflexible in approach. Many in the universities were also doubtful whether management was an appropriate field of study at university level and many academics perceived management studies as having lower status than more traditional disciplines. As R W Revans expressed it in 1956: 'Some universities still doubt whether industrial management provides the scope for students to participate in the advancement of knowledge or the pursuit of truth'.(4) This degree of mutual suspicion was reduced a little as quantitative methods became more widespread in use in industry in the late 1950's and the use of such techniques helped to bring industry and the universities somewhat closer together.

It was the early 1960's that the pace of development began to increase. The Robbins Report(5) (1963) had recommended that Britain should establish two postgraduate business schools and, in the same year, Lord Franks proposed that these should be established at London and Manchester.(6) In setting up these schools as postgraduate institutions, the decision had been made not to follow the European system of developing a cadre of potential senior managers by the provision of broad-based first degree courses at prestigious universities. The decision that remained was whether to recommend that the new schools should follow the North American model of management education (as exemplified by the Harvard Business School or the School of Industrial Management at the Massachusetts Institute of Technology) and concentrate greater attention on the development of young graduates destined to become the senior managers of the future, or to follow the pattern emerging in Britain which gave at least equal importance to the task of providing post-experience management training. Franks recommended that the new schools should develop both postgraduate and post-experience activities. He also suggested that these schools should have a high level of independence within their parent institutions, should foster collaboration between industry and the academic world and should set out to become international centres for excellence. It should be noted that both London and Manchester Business Schools departed from Franks' recommendation that their postgraduate courses should last one year. Following the American pattern both schools deemed it essential to develop two year programs (twenty-one months) in order to reach the standard thought to be appropriate.

Following the Franks Report, an appeal by the Foundation for Management Education led to over 350 companies subscribing £5 million. These funds were used to provide half the cost of construction and half the running costs of the London and Manchester Business Schools for a period of seven years. (The other half of the costs was met by government). In line with Lord Franks' recommendation that the establishment of the new major business schools should not preclude the growth and development of management development activities at other centres, more modest support was provided by the Foundation for other institutions. £420,000 was provided to fund developments at the universities of Durham, Edinburgh, Glasgow, London (London School of Economics and Imperial College) and Manchester, and at the Royal College of Science and Technology, Glasgow (now Strathclyde University), the Birmingham College of Advanced Technology (now Aston University) and the Regent Street Polytechnic (now the Polytechnic of Central London). Among other grants given at this time, funds were provided for Ashridge Management College to develop research and some new course development; to the

Roffey Park Institute to develop specialist courses on the human aspects of management and to Cranfield to develop its School of Management.

THE CURRENT SITUATION

Although there is little doubt that there is room for substantial improvement in the provision of management education and training in Britain, considerable growth has taken place in such activities during the past quarter of a century. It has been estimated that, in 1985, more than 100 universities, polytechnics and colleges provided programs for some 70,000 people enrolled on a wide range of business or management courses. In addition, 131,000 participant-weeks of 'open' management development courses were completed in the same year and it may be assumed that a somewhat greater number of participant-weeks of 'in-company' programs were also held. When considering these figures, however, it should be borne in mind that the United Kingdom has some three million managers and a great deal needs to be done to raise their level of management education to that achieved by their counterparts in other advanced nations.

The developments that have taken place have not, of course, been even and the situation in the various sectors can be summarised as follows.

Post-Graduate Management Education

The major business schools
The London and Manchester Business Schools produce 270 MBA graduates each year which means they have not yet achieved the output of postgraduates set for them in 1963. They have, however, experienced cuts in their funding from government (which currently stands at around 30 per cent of turnover) and both have had to develop more full-cost post-experience programs than had been planned originally. London, with its prestigious location and impressive buildings, has attracted some well-known scholars to its faculty. Some of the research findings emanating from the School receive a great deal of media coverage and this publicity has helped to establish a claim for it to be recognised as an international centre of excellence. Manchester is also highly regarded, is generally perceived by those in industry and commerce as

adopting a more practical approach than London, and is particularly well known for its joint development activities. Despite their achievements, these schools have not, at any rate as yet, achieved the same degree of prestige as some leading American schools. This may be due to their relatively new foundation. It should also be noted that, by international standards, both schools are small and their staff cover a range of activities - postgraduate and post-experience - which, in many overseas schools, would be areas of specialisation. Both schools, and particularly London, have attracted considerable criticism. Beginning with the Owen Report in 1971,(7) graduates of these institutions have been accused of being too theoretical, aggressive, ambitious and thus difficult to integrate within organisations. Many of these criticisms, albeit in a more muted form, have also been levelled at MBA graduates from other institutions.

Other university business schools
Since 1965 there has been an enormous growth in the provision of university MBA and taught masters degrees in the various functional areas of management (e.g. operational research or industrial relations). Thirty-one of Britain's universities (including the Open University and the Cranfield Institute of Technology) now provide programs in management and business studies. In 1985, their total output of MBA graduates and those who had completed specialist taught degree courses at the masters level in specialist functional areas of management was in the region of 2400. (This figure contains some 900 overseas students, thus making the output of UK graduates approximately 1500). The largest school, in terms of output of MBA graduates, is the Cranfield School of Management. Cranfield offers twelve months full-time and twenty-four months part-time MBA programs and produces more than 200 MBA graduates each year. Like London and Manchester, this school has no undergraduate activities. Its support from government (currently 15 per cent of turnover) is about half that received by London and Manchester.

Interesting developments are taking place at a number of schools, some of which are growing very quickly. Warwick, for example, has developed two consortium MBA's. One is run with Jaguar, Dunlop Aviation, GEC and Massey Ferguson; the other with BP, NatWest Bank, Coopers and Lybrand and the West

Midlands Police. The same school is also heavily involved in distance-learning activities. The City University Business School offers a modified consortium-style MBA with individual programs tailored to meet the needs of both individual students and their employers. Lancaster is working with British Airways on a two year part-time 'in company' MBA program which will be taken by about 50 people each year. This has been designed to develop high potential people in middle management roles in order to provide a pool of senior managers with the education and experience to lead the airline in the future. Bath runs an MBA program for British Aerospace and Henley runs a similar degree program for Shell. Durham has developed a considerable reputation for the work carried out in the development of small firms. The Open University Business School, which began in 1984, currently has about 7000 people taking its distance-learning courses and plans to begin offering an MBA program in 1989. This school also expects to be training 20,000 managers each year within five years.

A major difficulty faced by most, if not all, of these university business schools is the tension experienced by their academic staff in being assessed by groups with totally different value systems. To advance their academic careers, for example, they are expected to undertake and disseminate research to the standards of academic rigour achieved by other university departments. Unfortunately, this frequently leads to research studies with little relevance to problems faced by managers in the real world and where the chance of applying any findings are minimal. At the same time, however, they are expected to be seen as practical and relevant to the worlds of industry and commerce. To attempt to pursue these dual goals - academic and professional - together with a mixture of undergraduate, postgraduate and post-experience teaching, and sometimes a large administrative load, is obviously likely to result in considerable problems for those concerned.

The public sector
The biggest growth in postgraduate work in management education has taken place in the polytechnics and colleges. Many of the major polytechnics and some colleges offer MBA and specialist masters programs and, from a low base in 1965, they now produce around 1000 graduates each year. Developments are taking place similar to those in the

universities although the prime emphasis is on part-time programs. Oxford Polytechnic, for example, is working with W H Smith in the provision of an MBA program which combines 'in company' work with additional studies. Middlesex Polytechnic is working with Sutcliffe Catering to offer an MBA in the hospitality field. Brighton, Manchester and North East London Polytechnic are all involved in action-learning projects leading to masters degrees.

In an attempt to co-ordinate the development of non-university high level management education activities in the public sector, twelve regional management centres were set up by the Secretary of State for Education and Science between 1971 and 1978. Such centres were expected to be the point of further growth, to act as resource centres for the institutions in the regions and to develop closer collaboration with industry and commerce. They were be-devilled by a number of problems. Their funding base was uncertain. They covered large areas, some of which had a number of local education authorities - some of which might have different political persuasions and not be keen to co-operate - and, finally, one suspects that sometimes the management educators concerned were not particularly enthusiastic in co-operating with colleagues from other institutions. Most of the centres have ceased to exist, but some are still active and appear to be well regarded in their particular regions. The roles of these surviving regional management centres, however, seem to differ from one another and they do not appear to operate in the ways which were originally envisaged.

A comparatively recent development in the polytechnics has been the establishment of business schools. These new schools have utilised the staff of the primarily undergraduate business and accounting studies departments (which are well-established and highly regarded) in the provision of management education programs at the postgraduate level.

The independent sector

Although it is regarded as an independent institution, because of its postgraduate work carried out in conjunction with Brunel University, Henley Management College receives (via Brunel University) an earmarked block grant from the University Grants Committee. Henley has offered part-time MBA, MPhil and PhD programs since 1973 and these postgraduate activities represent an area of considerable growth in the College's activities. It has been estimated, for example, that in 1988 graduate studies programs will represent 42 per cent of Henley's income. Shell is working with the College in setting up a company-based MBA program for 80 of its managers in the current year. Henley is an important centre for distance learning and currently has some 400 distance learning students in Singapore, 350 in Hong Kong, 150 in Malaysia and 40 in both Finland and Holland.

Ashridge Management College is launching its first postgraduate program, which will lead to the award of an MBA degree of the City University, in 1988. This program will combine residential periods at Ashridge with action learning projects in the students organisations. As might be expected at this early stage of its development, the numbers involved are small.

In the light of such diversity - full-time or part-time; residential or non-residential; university, polytechnic or independent centre; one year or two year; 'general management' or 'specialist' programs; MBA taken immediately after completion of first degree or MBA taken after ten years' management experience - it will come as no surprise to learn that many British employers are bewildered by or ambivalent about MBA graduates. The problems they face have been well-documented by Kate Ascher(8) who points out that perceptions of the MBA program are unclear, that admissions performance criteria at some schools are loose and that increasing proportions of MBA graduates are going into finance and consulting industries. A more positive view is to be found in the report by Berry on a survey carried out of 536 MBA graduates drawn from the membership of the Business Graduates Association.(9) Berry notes that 56 per cent of his sample had first or upper second degrees (87 per cent with first or second class honours). Although 16 per cent were employed in banking and financial services and 14 per cent were in management consulting, there was a wide dispersion of other graduates through many sectors of the UK economy. Although the average age of this sample was under forty, 67 per cent reported themselves to be at senior managerial levels in their organisations and 33 per cent claimed to be at senior general management level. Berry reports that the increase in salary gained by graduates on obtaining the MBA degree (i.e. the increase in salary in the job immediately after graduation related to the salary earned prior to beginning the course) was 60 per cent. Although he cautioned that the salary levels of his sample were probably some fifteen per cent high, the average reported salary after gaining the MBA degree was £30,053 and the average value of benefits was £13,150, making up an annual remuneration package of £43,000, with the upper quartile approaching £50,000.

Three hundred and sixty one of these five hundred and sixty one graduates reported that the possession of the MBA degree was of very high or high value to them in their careers. As they had been promoted three times on average, this would appear to confirm that they had indeed made effective career progression. On the other hand, the response rate for this survey was only 18 per cent and it could well be the case that only the more successful returned the questionnaire. The importance these graduates attach to the value of their qualification may also be taken to reflect a degree of satisfaction on the part of their employers (60 per cent of which were British domestic companies) with these MBA graduates. Some interesting insights into the process of elite formation in British society are also provided by Berry's findings that MBA graduates who had attended public schools (i.e. private schools) received average salaries of £36,158 whilst the remainder received average salaries of £29,211; MBA graduates who held first degrees from Oxford or Cambridge received annual salaries of £37,385 and £34,353 respectively; women MBA graduates were paid substantially less than their male colleagues and, finally, those with an arts degree reported average salaries of £30,873 whereas those with a first degree in a science subject reported average salaries of £28,641.

Undergraduate Management Education

The Constable/McCormick Report noted that the total annual output of first degrees in business and management from all sectors was in the region of 4500 in 1985, about 5 per cent of which were non-EEC students. Some 25 per cent were produced by 23 universities and the remainder came from 41 polytechnics and colleges. The Report observes that many universities still favour the more traditional academic subject of economics, nevertheless the provision of courses in this discipline had not increased since 1972, whereas business and management studies programs have experienced a growth from 16 to 23. Although these courses were developed by the polytechnics, many universities have abandoned their traditional commerce programs and now offer business and management studies degrees. A particularly well-regarded undergraduate program is that offered by the University of Bath. This extends for four years and includes two six-month periods working in a company. The University of Glasgow is to join this group of universities in 1988 when it will offer a new first degree in Business Administration and it has been reported that the University of Oxford is also considering setting up a first degree course in this field.

About 25 per cent of applications for all polytechnic degree courses are for Business and Management Studies. In 1988 the total was 11,700 which represented an increase of 6.5 per cent on the previous year. In the university sector, applications for Business and Management Studies made this field the third (after law and medicine) most sought after program of study. In 1987 the total number of applications was 6,040 which represented an increase of 10.3 per cent on the previous year. Some indication of the value employers attribute to these courses is shown by the fact that the unemployment rate for the graduates of first degree business programs is only a little more than half of the average level.

Post-Experience Management Education

It has already been noted from the Constable Report that, in 1985, British managers completed at least 131,000 participant-weeks of open' management courses and probably rather more provision was made in respect of 'in company' programs, which, in recent years, have experienced considerable growth. Together, these represent a provision of about 0.6 days per year for each manager. Universities, polytechnics and colleges provided 62 per cent of these courses; private sector organisations 30 per cent; professional institutes 6 per cent and management consultants 2 per cent.

Unlike undergraduate and postgraduate education, activities in the post-experience field of management education are not normally subject to the scrutiny of boards of studies or external examiners but are subject to the demands of the market place. Both have their advantages and disadvantages. In attempting to be academically rigorous the former may stress, for example, areas such as quantitative analysis, whereas the latter may pander to the needs of some managers for lectures with high entertainment value. Some critics suggest that much of the work undertaken in post-experience management education is really remedial education overcoming deficiencies in the basic education received by British managers before embarking on their careers. In the experience of the writer, the courses provided range from excellent, innovative and challenging programs which meet all the demands of client organisations to some very doubtful offerings indeed. The tendency for organisations to send their most senior managers to European and American business schools to attend management development programs continues. This reflects the greater prestige enjoyed by such institutions and the opportunities attendance at such courses provide for the participants to meet managers from other countries and to develop an international perspective. The provision of in-house management training is also substantial: the Handy Report estimates that at least 40 British companies have their own management training centre.

THE FUTURE

At the time of writing (early 1988) it would appear that management education in Britain is poised for considerable growth in all sectors. The publication of the Handy and Constable/McCormick reports alerted decision-makers to many of the problems faced and these are being dealt with at senior levels. Under the aegis of the Foundation for Management Education, the Confederation of British Industry and the British Institute of Management, a Council of Management Education and Development has been formed under the chairmanship of Mr R P Reid, the Chairman of Shell UK. This initiative is supported by Government and the academic world. Major developments under consideration include the following.

Establishment of the Charter Group

In order to promote high standards of modern management practice and business skills at all levels
a Charter Group of Companies is to be established.
This group (which has already attracted support
from 100 companies including British Aerospace,
GKN, Grand Metropolitan, National Freight Consortium, Rank Xerox, RTZ and J Sainsbury) will promise
to follow a Management Charter embodying principles
and undertakings regarding work practices and the
development of skills which leading exponents of
good management would expect to achieve or better.
The basic aim of this Code of Practice will be to
increase the quantity and quality of management
education and development in Britain and thus
enhance the competitiveness of British business.

The Chartered Manager

The Council of Management Education and Development
has also proposed that a new professional institute
- the Institute of Chartered Managers - should be
set up to administer a new professional qualification - Chartered Manager. Such a qualification
would be awarded on the basis of both on-the-job
development and experience and appropriate, timely
inputs of formal training. It is planned to
establish the new Institute by September, 1988 and
for it to receive a Royal Charter by the end of the
same year.
    Although the aim to offer managers the same
prestige in society as other professionals is
laudable, clearly there are many difficulties to be
overcome in the setting up of sufficiently rigorous
standards for an award to be given on the basis of
experience as well as formal examinations. This
development is still in its early stages, however,
and it is likely that the award will become more
closely synchronised with the existing provisions
for management education as discussion continues.

Proposed Diploma in Business Studies

Both of the recently published reports recommend
the introduction of a new diploma course to be
undertaken by young people aspiring to a managerial
career, whether they be in industry, the public
sector or commerce. This course, which would prob-

ably be part-time, would include basic 'managerial' subjects such as accounting and finance, interpersonal skills, management of people, industrial relations, economics, statistics and quantitative techniques, computing and information systems, marketing and operations management. Constable recommends that the eventual target student throughput for such courses should be 35,000 per year. Handy proposed that such a course should be the first stage of a two part qualification scheme. Thus completion of such a diploma would become a pre-requisite for either entry into an MBA degree program or could be used by the business professional institutes as an integral part of their own qualification schemes.

MBA Degree

The Constable Report recommends that, in order to meet the nation's requirements for senior functional and general managers (estimated to be 17,500 each year), the annual intake of MBA students should be increased to 5000 after five years and 10,000 by the end of the century. In order to achieve these targets, the Report recommends the use of distance-learning methods and it also supports the growth of part-time and consortium style MBA programs.

These figures may be ambitious in the light of the suspicion many of those in industry and commerce display in connection with business masters graduates. Although demand for them is high, relatively few employers are prepared to sponsor students on these postgraduate programs and many question the appropriateness of such courses. Frequent complaints are made about the high salary and career expectations of MBA graduates and, as Kate Ascher concluded, it may still be too early to decide whether or not the decision to translate this American model to Britain was a wise one. It is certainly the case, as Berry has shown that many individuals benefit enormously from such programs, but the demand for their services could remain constant or even diminish should the availability of high calibre first degree graduates and holders of the new Diploma in Business Administration become more plentiful.

Certainly, a number of factors combine to make it essential that the form of existing MBA programs be reviewed. When, for example, holders of the proposed new diploma course or graduates with a first degree in business or management studies seek to pursue the MBA program their requirements are likely to differ considerably from the MBA students at the present time. What may be called for in future years may be a range of MBA programs meeting various requirements. Thus, the MBA with a general management orientation may need to continue for aspiring chief executives and general managers, but there could be a demand for more specialised MBA courses with a core of general management subjects but allowing more specialised study in a part of the program for potential senior functional managers. Modes of delivery may also change. Constable noted that, in 1984/85, there were over 4000 part-time postgraduate students in management studies compared with just over 3000 full-time students. It is to be expected that organisations may be increasingly reluctant to release their high calibre young managers for one or two years and, similarly, these young people may prefer to continue working and to pursue their studies on a part-time basis. Such changes provide enormous challenge and opportunities to educational institutions.

Some light on such changes have been shown in a recently published report(10) on a survey of the management education practices of major, successful European companies. The report suggests that these leading-edge organisations are making determined efforts to ensure that their management training activities are more relevant to their business needs. These companies used business schools to enable their managers to gain academic qualifications; to obtain access to networks outside the organisations; and to be exposed to new ideas. Nevertheless, many (as it happens, particularly non-British companies) were sceptical about the value of business school education. They suggested that business schools could become more effective by working more closely with companies in developing programs to meet specific needs; by encouraging academic staff to act as change agents in organisational development activities; and by adjusting their modes of delivery to emphasise the needs of the learner and particular problems.

To cope with these developments, it will be likely that the present range of institutions providing management education will become more specialised. Some will concentrate on 'general management' type programs; others will offer 'specialist' MBA courses and a few will concentrate on distance-learning. Constable proposed that there should be larger management schools, some of which should seek to develop outstanding international reputations. Similarly, 'The Economist' in 1983 concluded that the quality of postgraduate business in Britain would improve if resources were more concentrated.(11) ('The Economist' proposed that Henley/Brunel, Cranfield, London and Manchester should be among the survivors). There is evidence that this trend can already be discerned. Kate Ascher, for example, pointed out that a high proportion of the companies that actively recruit graduates do so only at London, Manchester and Cranfield. Similarly, Berry found that the graduates of these three schools were 'significantly more successful than the graduates of other management schools in the United Kingdom'. These three centres are all large by British standards (approximately 40-60 faculty members) and none is involved in undergraduate activities.

Undergraduate Education

In recent years, a number of initiatives have been taken to make students in schools aware of the challenges associated with careers in industry and commerce. The fact that the number of university applications for courses in business and management studies now comes second only to law and medicine may be seen as evidence that such initiatives have met with some success and that social attitudes towards managerial careers are changing. Constable recommends that undergraduate places in business and management studies in the universities, poly- technics and colleges, should be allowed to expand up to 50 per cent if there are sufficiently well- qualified young people seeking places. Such an increase implies an output of 7000 a year by 1995.

Post-Experience Management Education

Handy has recommended that British companies should commit themselves to providing five days training or education per manager per year and a Charter Group of companies committing themselves to this and similar practices has been established. Already this group includes such organisations as British Aerospace, British Airways, GKN, Grand Metropoli- tan, National Freight Corporation, Rank Xerox, RTZ and J Sainsbury. Because of the high proportion of managers in Britain who have received no training whatsoever, it is to be expected that post-experience management training activities will continue vigorously, particularly in the field of in-company training.

CONCLUSIONS

For many years, business schools and other providers of management education have been accused of providing programs which take little account of the needs of employers or of the skills required by managers in carrying out their roles. Although the work of researchers such as Rosemary Stewart(12), Mintzberg(13) and Kotter(14) have provided considerable insight into the nature of managerial work, remarkably little is known about the particular skills or competencies required by managers in different specialist functions, operating at various levels of organisations or in enterprises with particular cultures. As a result, most management development programs are broad in perspective. Discovering what competencies are required by managers in different situations could become a central area for research and the findings of any such work important for the future of management development activities.

The developments described above will, if implemented, call for large numbers of additional management teachers. It has been estimated that the numbers involved could reach 1000 in the next few years and a further 2-3000 by the mid-1990's. The present system of training, based on two points of entry - in the 20's often with a PhD degree or at a later age for those with practical experience of management - is clearly inadequate and needs to be improved radically. Constable recommends that additional resources (at least £2 million and possibly as much as £5 million per year for a minimum period of 10 years) should be allocated for this training of management trainers. Such an injection of funds and innovative training methods could do much to improve the general standard of management training. Constable also recommended that 'high fliers' from industry and commerce should be encouraged to undertake part-time teaching commitments in the field of management education. This already occurs to a limited extent, but greater involvement by practising managers would do much to facilitate closer links between the worlds of education and industry and commerce.

Equally important for the future success of management education and training will be the ways in which those engaged in these activities are organised. Many reports on the establishment of business schools recommend that these centres should be relatively independent of their parent institutions. (In recent years, there have been suggestions that business schools in Britain should be privatised(15) although support for such a move has been limited). Most British management schools in universities and polytechnics are much closer to what may be called an academic model of organisation than they are a professional school. They tend to emphasise the discipline that underlies issues and value publications by staff in academic journals. A few schools, however, are much closer to a professional model where activities such as joint work with client organisations, papers in professional journals and high-level consultancy assignments are well-regarded. It is likely that, over the next few years, more polarisation of these institutions will occur with those primarily concerned with postgraduate and post-experience work moving closer to the professional model, whilst those primarily involved in undergraduate work may move closer to the academic model. Such developments have implications for the recruitment and management of staff, methods of payment, career progression and so on.

The era of intense competition and rapid change faced by British industry and commerce has made many people aware of the critical importance of management and leadership enabling organisations to function in a world which is no longer stable and ordered. As a result, never before has the climate for developments in the field of management education and training been more favourable. As has been shown, rapid changes are beginning to take place and it is likely that management development and education in Britain will expand and undergo considerable change in the next ten to twenty years.

NOTES

1. John Constable and Roger McCormick, The Making of British Managers, British Institute of Management and Confederation of British Industry, London (1987).

2. Charles Handy, et al. The Making of Managers, National Economic Development Office, London (1987).

3. Colonel Lord Urwick, Education for Management, Report of a Special Committee appointed by the Ministry of Education, London HMSO (1947).

4. R.W. Revans, quoted in Malcolm Peel, Management Development and Training. A Survey of Current Policy and Practice, British Institute of Management and Professional Publishing Ltd. London (1984).

5. Lord Robbins, Higher Education, Report of the Committee, London HMSO, 4 vols Cmnd 2154, (1963).

6. Lord Franks, British Business School, Staple Press (1963).

7. Trevor Owen, Business School Programmes: the Requirements of British Manufacturing Industry, British Institute of Management (1971).

8. Kate Ascher, Masters of Business? The MBA and British Industry, Hartridge House Europe, London (1984).

9. A.J. Berry, The Business Masters Graduate in the UK Economy, Manchester Business School, Business Graduate Association and Egon Zehnder International (March 1987).

10. Kevin Barham, Jim Fraser and Laura Heath, 'Management for the Future', Foundation for Management Education and Ashridge Management College (March 1988).

11. 'Educating Britain's bosses', The Economist, (September 17, 1983).

12. Rosemary Stewart, Managers and the Jobs, Macmillan, London (1967).

13. H. Mintzberg, The Nature of Managerial Work, Harper & Row, New York (1973).

14. John Kotter, The General Manager, Free Press, New York (1982).

15. Brian Griffiths and Hugh Murray, Whose Business, Institute of Economic Affairs (1985).

Chapter Four

MANAGEMENT EDUCATION IN AUSTRALIA
William Byrt

INTRODUCTION

Australia has been described as a 'small (in terms
of population not area), rich industrial society.'
The description probably remains true despite the
current economic downturn and the problems beset-
ting manufacturing industry.

The population is comparatively small, approximately 16 million, and the area large just over 7.6
million square kilometres, about the size of main-
land USA excluding Alaska.

Australia is not a mirror image of any other
country or nation. Until the end of World War II,
the population was principally British-Irish in its
origins, with a small population of aborigines.
Since then, however, there has been a steady influx
of migrants from other European countries and, more
recently, from Asia. Today, one person in four is
either a migrant who has arrived in the country
since the War or the child of one.

Australia has been dominated by what Geoffrey
Blainey has called 'the tyranny of distance'(1). It
measures approximately 4,000 kilometres from east
to west and 3,000 from north to south and has a
coastline of 36.7 thousand kilometres. Settled
originally from Europe and drawing its political
institutions, culture and ideologies from there,
its east coast is 17,000 kilometres from London and
about 12,000 from the west coast of the United
States. Almost 90 per cent of its population are
urban dwellers, mostly on the rim, the coastal
regions, particularly the 'boomerang coast' stret-

ching from the north-east, through the south-east to the south. Sixty per cent of the population live in New South Wales and Victoria which cover only just over 13 per cent of the area of the country. Approximately 40 per cent of the population live in Sydney or Melbourne, the capital cities of New South Wales and Victoria, respectively.

Australia's economy was originally based on primary production, particularly wool, meat, wheat and sugar and on mining. These industries are still the largest exporters. During this century, a manufacturing industry was developed with the help of tariff protection. Manufacturing and service industries - transport, finance, education, government services - are the major employers.

There is a comparatively high degree of foreign ownership of Australian manufacturing and mining industries. This has been principally British and American but, in recent years, there has been an increase in Asian and Middle-eastern investment in Australia.

The political situation is stable, government in the Commonwealth and States being shared by Liberal/National (conservative) and Labor (right-wing or moderate social democratic) governments. Australian is a western-type democracy, its political institutions being based on a mixture of the British Westminster and American federal systems. Politically, Australia may be described as a liberal, democratic, interventionist, welfare state. It is highly-unionised, trade unions enjoy a good deal of industrial and political power, the latter through the Australian Labor Party with which most unions are affiliated.

The culture was derived originally from Europe, particularly Britain. There has, in recent years, been a growth in American cultural influence. There has been some increase in Asian influence and some rhetoric that Australia is an Asian country - Indonesia is its nearest major neighbour and about 40 per cent of Australia's trade is with South-east Asia and Japan. There has even been some attempt to spread the influence of aboriginal culture. However, culturally the country still remains largely European.

Management education in Australia, as in most countries, has been carried out at a number of levels and in a variety of forms. A primary categorisation being between award and non-award courses.

Award courses involve the assessment of the performance of students by means of examinations, assignments, theses or dissertations, or a combination of these. Successful students being awarded degrees, diplomas or certificates.

The most prestigious courses culminate in the award of a postgraduate degree, either at doctoral or masters' level. The most common of the latter being the Master of Business Administration (MBA). Other awards are made at bachelor, diploma or certificate level. Some management education is provided as part of courses in such disciplines as engineering, architecture, building or applied science.

Non-award courses do not entail assessment of students, so that nobody 'fails'. Such courses may be 'in-house' being provided for employees of particular companies or public services (Commonwealth or State), government departments or instrumentalities or they may be 'open', being offered by educational institutions or by management consultants. Open courses, as the term indicates, are open to any suitable persons who can pay or, more commonly, whose employing organisations can pay, the fairly substantial fees charged. Those who complete such courses are usually awarded a document certifying that they have completed, not 'passed' the course.

Australian management education prior to the 1950s was largely indigenous, although foreign models were undoubtedly drawn upon. From the 1950s onwards, it constituted an aspect of what has been called educational imperialism, part of the management education movement emanating principally from the United States.

THE NATIVE GROWTH

Education and training for managers which developed in Australia prior to the 1950s did not bear the title management education. It took a variety of forms and was provided by various institutions.

Commerce degrees offered by Australian universities were among the earliest ventures into management education, without that term being used. The University of Melbourne's degree of Bachelor of Commerce provides an early example of such a course. It is particularly interesting to the historian of management education for a number of reasons. The first post-experience, residential course in management conducted by an Australian University was established within the University's Faculty of Economics and Commerce. The Graduate

School of Business Administration, later to become the Graduate School of Management, was established within the Faculty. The foundation Dean of the Faculty, Professor Douglas Berry Copland, became the foundation Principal of the Australian Administrative Staff College.

The Faculty of Economics and Commerce, originally entitled the Faculty of Commerce, was established in October 1924. The first students being admitted at the commencement of the 1925 academic year. A degree of Bachelor of Commerce was offered. Subsequently, the Faculty offered an Honours degree and degrees of Master and Doctor of Commerce and provided supervision for candidates for the Doctorate of Philosophy.

The primary basis of the original Commerce degree was economics. The objective of the course was to provide tertiary education for persons employed in 'commerce and business'. In fact, they were usually employees of large organisations in the public and private sectors - government departments and instrumentalities, banks, oil companies and so on. Most were part-time students. Even by 1939, the percentage of full-time undergraduates in the degree course was still low at 24 per cent. Post war conditions saw an increase in the proportion of full-time students who are now in the majority.

Commerce students have tended to be persons holding, or aspiring to hold positions of accountant, economist, manager or teacher.

In his inaugural lecture Copland thanked men of commerce whose interest in higher commercial education had paved the way for the work of the School of Commerce. He stated that commercial education was likely to be much more successful if it sprang from the needs of industry and was supported by businessmen. These comments indicate that the roots of the School of Commerce were seen to lie in an interaction between university and business worlds, an interaction which would provide educated young graduates to the business community.

There was, from the beginning, a heavy emphasis on the study of economics. Subsequently, the study of accountancy and business law became important and completion of the degree, with appropriate subjects in those fields, one method of obtaining Associateship of the Australian Society of Accountants.

Today, the disciplines taught by the Faculty's departments are:

Accounting
Business Administration
Business Law
Economic History
Economics, including Urban and
  Regional Economics
Industrial Relations
Marketing
Quantitative Methods

In 1983, the Graduate School of Business Administration ceased to be a Department of the Faculty and the Graduate School of Management became a separate School of the University.

An interest in management training developed in Australia during World War II. The Institute of Industrial Administration, later The Australian Institute of Management, was set up. In addition to providing a forum for discussion of management problems, the Institute provided short courses in various aspects of management. These were usually held outside normal working hours and the lecturers were drawn from either educational institutions or from industry. Most of the training in management provided was directed at persons at the first-line of management, supervisors. Middle and senior managers were considered to be too busy to attend courses or not to need any training; they had learnt to manage by managing!

Technical colleges, later to become Institutes of Technology and subsequently Colleges of Advanced Education (CAE) and of Tertiary and Further Education (TAFE), provided courses in supervision. During the war, the training of supervisors to enable them to manage better the increasing number of employees, often inexperienced, in the growing war industries was attacked through technical college courses and government-sponsored Training Within Industry (TWI). Initially, there were three standardised TWI programs, the titles of which are self-explanatory: Job Instruction (JI), Job Methods (JM), Job Relations (JR). Later, a fourth Job Safety (JS) was added, allegedly as a sop to the trade union movement.

With the cessation of hostilities, the interest in management training and education continued to grow. There were parallel developments in Sydney and Melbourne in the 1950s to provide something more prestigious than the technical college programmes and the evening courses of the Institutes of Management and other professional bodies. These will be examined in more detail later.

The technical colleges moved to upgrade their offerings. In 1951, at a conference of technical colleges' management schools, a standardised syllabus of studies was established for the management certificate throughout Australia. This course usually extended over four years of part-time study and covered such topics as economic background, management principles and techniques of organisation, statistical method, legal and psychological aspects of business, human relations in management and the personnel, financial, production and other aspects of management. In Melbourne the course was developed to lead to a diploma in management, the diploma course extending over six years. Similar courses were conducted in various States, although no common standards for a diploma were established. Another development was that, in the technical colleges, efforts were made to give people doing technical diploma courses at least an introduction to some aspects of management. At one college, for example, two hours a week was devoted to management studies in the last year of all diploma courses.

EDUCATIONAL IMPERIALISM

The post-war development of management education constituted part of the world-wide expansion of the influence of the United States.

The United States came out of World War II with an enhanced reputation for industrial and military efficiency. This was attributed to a number of factors: the nation's stable, democratic political system; its affluence; its natural resources; its size in area and population; its educational institutions; its standard of management.

With the cessation of hostilities, the United States commenced to intervene in other countries; to export to them food, capital, skills, equipment, ideas, ideology. This was done for a variety of reasons. Social, to try to do something to alleviate human misery. Economic, on the grounds that America could not remain prosperous in an economically depressed world. Political, as a counter to the other super-power, the Soviet Union.

One of the American exports was the system of management, referred to colloquially as part of 'American know-how'. The first managerial exports were managers and methods of management, followed by management education.

Australians had seen and admired American management during World War II; within Australia itself and in the nearby theatres of war. There was not another system to place on a pedestal. British management was not highly regarded by Australians and the German and Japanese 'miracles' had yet to occur. In the post-war period, American companies came to Australia, as they went to many other countries, to engage in developmental work: building refineries; mining; constructing roads, bridges, harbours and aerodromes. They brought with them managers, skilled workers and 'know-how'.

The curricula of American 'business schools' particularly Harvard, were adopted and adapted for Australian conditions and the so-called Harvard case-study method was taken-over as a major pedagogical technique. The degree of Master of Business Administration (MBA) developed as the archetypal postgraduate degree, awards of a lower level - bachelor, diploma and certificate - being modelled on it.

Non-award programs for experienced managers commenced to be conducted by bodies such as the Australian Administrative Staff College (based, however, on Henley, not Harvard), The Bankers' Administrative Staff College and various employing organisations, at first almost entirely in the public sector, for example, The Commonwealth Public Service Board and the Postmaster-General's Department (later divided into Telecom Australia and Australia Post).

Most students and observers of management education in Australia agree that, post-World War II, the climate was right for a 'great leap-forward'. The successful mobilisation of the nation's war effort had shown to many what could be achieved by efficient management. The nation was becoming more open to external influences. The era of 'the lucky country' was just beginning with its belief in unchecked economic growth and permanent affluence, a belief challenged later by the economic storms which hit the country. There was a somewhat uncritical belief that almost anything could be achieved through education, including management education.

There were two major developments in the 1950s. Melbourne University's first Summer School of Business Administration, a six-weeks' residential course for executives, was held during January-February 1956. The School was roughly modelled on the Harvard executive programs. The case-study method was introduced to Australia by Hal Craig, the only member of the original directing staff who had had any experience in management education for executives and who possessed a Harvard doctorate. The Australian Administrative Staff College, modelled on the Administrative Staff College at Henley-on-Thames, conducted its first course in 1957.

Although the Summer School was originally governed by a Board of Management responsible to the Council of the University, it had strong links with the Commerce Faculty. The foundation Vice-Principal, the senior academic, the Principal being a business executive, was Professor Don Cochrane, Sidney Myer Professor of Commerce. The other four members of the Directing Staff were Doug Hocking, a member of the Faculty, Myer Kangan, a public servant and part-time teacher in the Faculty, Hal Craig, a consultant later to become a Faculty member and Vic Gole, a practising accountant.

When John Willett became Sidney Myer Professor of Commerce and Business Administration (the Chair of Commerce having been re-named) in 1962, he took over the position of Vice-Principal and, over the next few years, the School came to be staffed almost entirely by members of the staff of the newly-formed Department of Commerce and Business Administration, a Department of the Faculty.

The Summer School has developed into the two Advanced Management Programs and one Program for Management Development (four weeks) conducted by the Graduate School of Management of the University of Melbourne. Over 3,000 executives have completed the University's programs since the first in 1956.

The major stimulation for the foundation of the Australian Administrative Staff College came from a Sydney solicitor Geoff Remington. In 1952 he began to canvass among his colleagues in Rotary the idea of an educational institution devoted to the education of managers. Originally, he had thought of a university department, faculty or institute. However, the University of Sydney showed little interest and he turned in another direction.

It was arranged for Noel Hall, the first Principal of the Administrative Staff College at Henley-on-Thames, to come to Australia for five weeks, three of which were spent in Sydney, in September 1954. He visited universities, institutions, associations, conferences and councils interested in management education and had discussions with managers and others. It was as a result of these discussions that the Australian sponsors decided that they would go ahead with an

Australian Administrative Staff College.

By February 1955, the College was formally incorporated as a company limited by guarantee. A governing council was set up by invitation and Essington Lewis, Chief General Manager of the Broken Hill Proprietary Company, invited to become Chairman. Professor Sir Douglas Copland, at that time Australian High Commissioner in Canada and previously Dean of Commerce in the University of Melbourne, was appointed Principal on 5th April 1956. A building was purchased, ironically, given the rivalry between Australia's two major cities, not in or near Sydney but at Mount Eliza on the shores of Port Phillip Bay about 50 kilometres from Melbourne and the College was set up there.

The first course of twelve weeks duration commenced in September 1957. The College has developed and expanded, the major courses held by it in 1986 being:

4 Advanced Management Programs	- 6 weeks
3 Senior Management Programs	- 4 weeks
4 Management Development Programs	- 4 1/2 weeks
1 ASEAN - Australian International Management Programs	- 2 weeks
The Corporate Strategy Series	

The original premises have been enlarged considerably by development and building and facilities are now available to organisations wishing to use the premises for courses and seminars.

The College is not affiliated with any other tertiary educational institution and does not receive government funding.

The pedagogical methods used at the Staff College aim at achieving a balance between case-studies, lectures, projects, seminars, syndicate-work and private study. An adaptation of the Henley syndicate method provides a distinctive contribution.

On each course, syndicates of eight members are formed, each being allocated a member of staff as a syndicate leader. The latter works closely with the syndicate during the duration of the course, acting as facilitator - 'guide, philosopher and friend', not necessarily teacher. If a staff member has experience in, knowledge of or ability in teaching a particular subject, he or she may be called upon to conduct formal classes in that area for the whole of the course members. The objective of the syndicate method is to enable members to work upon subjects with the objective of applying the information obtained to specific practical issues, that is, developing decision-making abilities rather than studying a subject for its own sake or to advance its boundaries.(2)

Management consultants also entered the field of management education during this period. For example, W.D. Scott, John P. Young and Geoffrey Beckingsale conducted courses for executives, sometimes using the services of a visiting American academic.

THE MBA MOVEMENT

What has been called 'the MBA Movement' developed in Australia as an offshoot of American educational imperialism. Postgraduate courses along the lines of those provided by American 'business schools', particularly Harvard, being provided by Australian tertiary institutions. The term 'business school' was new to Australia where the title 'business college' had been used for institutions providing commercial education in subjects such as typing and shorthand. Although some of the courses bore titles other than Master of Business Administration (MBA), they were similar in aim and content to that degree and MBA may be regarded as generic term covering a particular class of degree.

The first two Australian tertiary institutions to offer degrees of MBA were the Universities of Melbourne and New South Wales. Their programs commenced in 1963, the same year in which a degree of Master of Business Management was inaugurated at the University of Adelaide.

By 1970, when the Cyert Inquiry into Australian management education (to be considered later) was held, four Australian universities were offering 'MBA type' programs: Melbourne, New South Wales, Adelaide, Monash.

The University of Melbourne

In May 1957, the State Executive of the Victorian Liberal Party, the party in government in the State, had asked the University of Melbourne to investigate the steps necessary to establish a postgraduate School of Industrial and Business Research at the University. In June 1957, in response to this request, Professor Sir Alexander

Fitzgerald, Dean of the Faculty of Economics and Commerce, reported that an ideal arrangement would be a postgraduate school superimposed on a strong undergraduate one, conducting executive training courses as a by-product.

In October, the State Council of the Liberal Party recommended that a postgraduate School of Industrial Research should be set up and that the Summer School should expand, finance being provided from industry and business. Reference was made to a 'Harvard-type postgraduate School of Business Research which would also conduct executive training programmes'. It would appear that, despite the proposed name, what was envisaged was a teaching rather than a research institution.

In December, the Faculty of Economics and Commerce recommended the establishment of a Graduate School within the Faculty to offer a degree of Master of Business Administration, either one year full-time or two years' part-time and this was approved in principle by the Council of the University.

In 1961, the Sidney Myer Chair of Commerce was vacated by Don Cochrane who became Foundation Dean of Economics and Politics at Monash University, and was renamed the Sidney Myer Chair of Commerce and Business Administration.

John Willett, a Cambridge academic, was appointed to the Chair and took up duty in Melbourne on October 10th 1962. A decision was made to offer a two-year degree of Master of Business Administration (MBA). The Preliminary Year, could, and usually has been, taken on a part-time basis and spread over two years whereas the Final Year must be taken full-time. Application for admission to the course leading to the degree was open to university graduates of any faculty or holders of an equivalent qualification. To be admitted to the course, a candidate was required to show that he or she had had at least two years' experience in some public or private organisation. In fact, most candidates entering the Final Year have had at least five years' working experience.

The first candidates for the degree commenced their courses in Term 1, March 1963. The first group to complete the course, numbering seven, did so by the end of 1964. They had been able to complete the Preliminary Year in one year through being given exemptions in certain subjects.

The subjects of the original course may be compared with those offered in 1986:

Preliminary Year

1962	1986
Accounting & Finance	Finance & Control
Economic Structure & Policy	Economic Structure & Policy
Introduction to Business Statistics	Quantitative Analysis
	Management Computing
Engineering Study	
Business & Society	
	Organisational Behaviour

Final Year

1962	1986
Business Case Study	Business Policy
Business Organisation & Human Relations	Organisation Theory
	Industrial Relations
Quantitative Analysis	Decision Analysis
Economic Decision Analysis	Financial Management
	Marketing Management
	Current Issues in Management (non-examinable)
Research Report	Research Report

The rationale of the degree has been to furnish education in general management, not training in functional skills. No particular first-degree studies have been set as pre-requisites, it being considered that, by completing the Preliminary Year, each student has been brought to a satisfactory level in the basic areas of finance, economics, organisational behaviour, quantitative methods and the use of computers. Originally, no elective subjects were offered, all being compulsory excepting where an exemption was given. At one stage, each Final Year candidate was required to do two electives drawn from the fields of financial, marketing and personnel management, public administration and entrepreneurship. However, electives were subsequently abolished and in 1986 all subjects were compulsory excepting that, in Final Year, each student was required to do Business Policy and Marketing Management plus three of the other four examinable subjects.

The department headed by Willett was originally entitled the Department of Commerce and Business Administration of the Faculty of Economics and Commerce. It 1973, the Graduate School of Business Administration was formed by an amalgamation of the Department with the Summer School. In 1984, the Graduate School of Management was established as a School within the University, not as part of a Faculty. These Schools have been responsible for:

The supervision of candidates for the Doctorate of Philosophy in management.
Providing the course leading to the MBA.
Teaching undergraduate management subjects to students in the Faculty of Commerce and other Faculties.
Conducting executive programs.

Approximately 850 students completed the Melbourne MBA over the years 1964-1986, inclusive.

The University of New South Wales

In 1958, the Faculty of Commerce was established in the University of New South Wales, with chairs in Business Administration, Hospital Administration, Economics and Accounting. Neville Wills, at that time Manager of Commercial Research at the Broken Hill Proprietary Company Limited (BHP), and previously a lecturer in Government at the University of Sydney, was, at the end of 1960, offered the Foundation Professorship in Business Administration. He took up duties at the beginning of 1961 but did not commence to enrol postgraduate students until 1963, the same year as Melbourne. The degree was originally named Master of Administration but had been changed to MBA by the time that the first students graduated. The course could be done on either a full-time (two years) or part-time basis. The model on which the New South Wales course was originally based has been described as a mixture of Carnegie-Mellon (quantitatively-oriented) and Harvard (case-study oriented). In its developmental stages, the School made a good deal of use of part-time teachers, a number of whom were members of the Harvard Club centred in Sydney. Eventually, the New South Wales MBA became more Harvard than Carnegie-Mellon.
    The New South Wales School developed stronger relationships with the business community than did

its opposite number in Melbourne. This may have been assisted by Harvard Club links. Money was raised to fund two Chairs - one in Marketing and in one in Finance. In addition there was the original Chair of Organisational Behaviour.

Monash University

The Foundation Dean of the Faculty of Economics and Politics at Monash University, the second university to be established in Victoria, was Professor Donald Cochrane who had been the first Vice-Principal of Melbourne's Summer School.

A degree of Master of Administration, changed to Master of Business Administration at the beginning of 1987, was established at Monash in the Faculty of Economics and Politics shortly after the introduction of the MBA at Melbourne. There were a number of differences between the Melbourne and Monash degrees. The latter consisted of the equivalent of two years' full-time study plus a minor thesis. Few students pursued the degree on a full-time basis. It was described as a 'day release', as distinct from a full-time or part-time, course. That is, most classes were held during the day, not in the morning or evening as with the Preliminary Year of Melbourne's MBA. Working students needed to be granted leave from their employment to attend classes. The full content was not compulsory, a large number of optional subjects being offered.

Most subjects were not designed specifically for M Admin students but were also taken by undergraduates. Although a Chair of Administration was created it was not filled until 1969. Two Senior Lecturers headed the Administrative Studies unit.

The University of Adelaide

The University of Adelaide established in 1960, in its Department of Commerce, a Department of the Faculty of Economics, a postgraduate program leading to a degree of Master of Business Administration. Seminar courses for the degree were commenced in 1963. Financial support was provided by five large financial, commercial and industrial organisations.

The original proposal for the degree, made in July 1960, emphasised that it was intended not to provide training in administrative skills in the

91

functional areas of management, or to establish a school of business on the American pattern but rather to extend the work of existing university disciplines 'into those areas of business management which lend themselves to advanced academic analysis'. The degree was intended partly to meet the requirements of graduates of faculties other than Commerce who had taken up employment in commerce or industry and subsequently assumed managerial responsibilities and partly to provide advanced courses to economics graduates making their careers in business or the public services rather than in research or academic institutions.

Seminar-type courses were offered in six major areas:

Social and Political Institutions and Thought
Economic Institutions and Policy
Economic and Accounting Analysis
Business Statistics
Human Relations
Decision-making

Until comparatively recently, the Adelaide course had not developed to any great extent. It was probably overshadowed by the MBA offered by the Elton Mayo School of Management at the neighbouring South Australian Institute of Technology.

THE CYERT INQUIRY

There have been two major landmarks in the history of Australian management education, the Cyert Inquiry, 1970, and the Ralph Inquiry, 1980-1982.

Tertiary education in Australia is financed principally by the Commonwealth Government, tuition fees not being paid by local students at government-funded institutions. There has been some funding by individuals and organisation and some experiments with 'user-pays' programs targeted mostly at foreign students. Bond University, at present being developed in Queensland but not yet operating, is Australia's only private tertiary educational institution.

The management schools which developed during the 1960s felt that they were disadvantaged financially. They had arrived too late on the scene to benefit from the post-war boom in education and were attempting to grow in a period of financial cutback or decrement. They were competing against one another and, within their own institutions, with more firmly established departments or faculties, many of the members of which regarded management education as not constituting a 'true' academic discipline.

Various institutions lobbied governments and business with very limited success. The attitude of the latter, with a few exceptions, was that the financing of tertiary education was a matter for government and that generosity towards one institution would provoke claims from others which it would be difficult to refuse.

John Willett developed the 'two universities' policy', based on Britain's strategy of developing two 'schools of excellence' at London and Manchester respectively, while giving some financial support to other institutions. Willett undoubtedly envisaged that Australia's London and Manchester would be at the Universities of Melbourne and New South Wales.

The Commonwealth Government did what most democratic governments do when faced with a 'too hard' situation, one which it really does not understand, on which it has no clear policy and where any realistic decision will upset certain interests. It set up a committee of inquiry.

The Committee of Inquiry into postgraduate education for management (the Cyert Committee), which was appointed in November 1961, consisted of four Americans, three academics and one management consultant. Its chairman was Richard M Cyert, Dean of the Graduate School of Industrial Administration in Carnegie-Mellon University. One British academic was invited but he eventually declined. The Committee was asked to report on the availability of postgraduate education in Australia and to make recommendations for meeting future needs. Its members arrived in the country in February 1970 and the Committee reported to the Commonwealth Government on 22nd March of the same year.(3) In summary, it recommended that existing programs should be encouraged, although obviously it was not greatly impressed by them, and that one 'school of excellence' should be established and receive substantial government funding. That School to be at the University of New South Wales.

CYERT TO RALPH

At first it appeared that the recommendations of the Cyert Committee were not likely to be implemented. They lay fallow for about three years. A number of reasons have been advanced for this:

. The whole purpose of the exercise had been to make sure that no action was taken.
. The Commonwealth Liberal Government had more important things on its mind, including internal dissension, than management education.
. There had been opposition from Melbourne (the 'heartland of Liberalism') to setting up one national school of business administration in Sydney.

So nothing happened for three years. However, in 1973, rumours commenced to float about that the Whitlam Labor Government intended to implement the Cyert report.

It was implemented, the new school established within the University of New South Wales was called the Australian Graduate School of Management. It was to offer doctoral and masters' programs, the latter on a two-year full-time basis, and shorter non-degree, post-experience courses. A Board of Management, with substantial representation from outside the University, was established. All positions were advertised and no senior member of the academic staff of the existing school at the University of New South Wales was appointed to one. It has been said that none applied. The school commenced operations in 1977.(4)

The decade of the 1970s, the period between the Cyert and Ralph Committees, was one of bewilderment in management education in Australia. The general air of gloom was marked by a few initiatives. The major developments during the period, such as they were, probably occurred, as they had in the 1960s, at the Universities of Melbourne and New South Wales.

John Willett described the Cyert investigation as 'nearly the kiss of death for management education in Australia'. It damaged morale in the Melbourne School. It tainted the views of the business community about the Australian business education product and management education soon became highly fragmented with the action moving to smaller providers. He considered that the Cyert priority given to research, staff development and scholarship was not an appropriate or feasible strategy for Australia at the time - any more than it would have been if Wharton or Harvard had set out to initiate management education by this route.(5)

The decade of the 1970s was not one of retreat, in fact there were some gains. Despite the lack of support by government and business, developments in management education proceeded, if slowly, at a number of Universities and Colleges of Advanced Education.

At Melbourne, a policy of 'self-help', the generation of funds through executive programs, paid-off to some extent. The 'school of excellence', the Australian Graduate School of Management in the University of New South Wales, developed slowly. An Interim Board of Management was set up in 1974. Its Chairman was Gordon Jackson, General Manager of CSR Limited. Philip Brown, Professor of Accounting in the University of Western Australia was appointed as Director for a period of five years from June 1975. Its planned activities were:(6)

    Courses for Experienced Managers
    Masters Programme
    Doctoral Programme
    The Production of Australian
     Educational Materials
    Research

Its dominant model appears to have been Chicago with a heavy emphasis on research and the doctoral program.

It is probably not unfair to state that the AGSM, despite its label as a 'school of excellence', had not made a great impact on Australian management education until into the 1980s. The number of students, either on degree or executive courses, was not great. The offerings of the School were criticised as being 'too academic' and having a bias towards mathematically-based subjects.

Philip Brown's five-year appointment as Director finished in 1980 and he was succeeded by Jeremy Davis, a former management consultant. This appointment appears to have heralded a change in the strategy in the AGSM, its approach becoming more 'practical'.

THE RALPH COMMITTEE

Australia's second Committee of Inquiry into Management Education (the Ralph Committee) was set up in 1980, probably in response to Melbourne lobbying and general dissatisfaction among management educators with the results of the Cyert Committee. It commenced to function in May of that year and reported to the Commonwealth Minister for Education in April 1982. It was chaired by John Ralph, Deputy Managing Director, later Managing Director of CRA, the multi-national mining company. The other members were an academic, a management consultant and two top executives. All were Australian based. 'Big Business' was well represented.

The Ralph Committee was asked:

.   to examine the availability of courses in management education for middle and top management;
.   to assess the effectiveness of such courses in raising management standards and in meeting the needs of business Management Education in Australia enterprises;
.   to examine the manner of financing management education specifically including consideration of the question whether or not education for managers who are sponsored by business should be made self-supporting;
.   to examine the special needs of small business for management education; and
.   to make such recommendations to the Tertiary Education Commission as the Committee deems necessary in respect of the general nature and availability of courses in management education, including proposals for new courses.(7)

The Committee took the view that a government can not legislate for good education and that it (the Committee) should not attempt to prescribe curricula or methods of teaching. Its task was to attempt to ensure that adequate resources were available in the right places. It agreed that there was a limited demand in Australia for full-time award courses in management education but considered that some such courses should be provided.

The Committee's major stated concern was with the quality of award programs being offered.Quality was being prejudiced by an allocation of resources that resulted in staff and students being spread too thinly across too many institutions. Many institutions were seeking to deliver programs without the minimum resources necessary to provide the range and depth of subjects needed for high quality management education. In this environment, as institutions competed for students seeking management education, the temptation existed to compromise standards in order to maintain student numbers.

The Committee recommended three broad areas of action to improve the quality of management education in Australia:

. institutions should be organised and resources allocated in a way which would encourage and allow each institution to provide specific and complementary modes and forms of award management education. In addition, institutions should conduct non-award programs consistent with their areas of particular expertise;
. the level of interaction between tertiary institutions and the management community should be raised; and
. a number of specific steps should be taken to improve the quality of staff, students, and courses in all institutions providing management education.

It recommended a three-tier system:

> National Management Schools
> Regional Management Schools
> Other Tertiary Institutions

The mission of a national management school was seen as being to provide leadership for practitioners and academics in management throughout Australia. It would do this by providing actual and potential leaders of the practising management and academic communities with high quality education, ideas and concepts that helped them improve their performance throughout their careers. A national management school would achieve this mission through MBA programs with substantial full-time components, doctoral programs, major research, non-award courses, and other management development activities. These schools would be national in the sense of being schools of excellence and at the forefront of management education in the nation.

The mission of a regional management school would be to provide a broad spectrum of actual and potential managers with high quality programs that improve their managerial skills while they continue in their careers. Regional schools should achieve this mission through part-time MBA programs, non-award courses, other management development activities and research.

The mission of other tertiary institutions in management education was to provide the management community with wide access to a variety of programs meeting local needs to improve managerial skills. These institutions should achieve this mission through undergraduate courses and postgraduate diplomas for students with work experience, through non-award courses and through other management development activities.

THE PRESENT SITUATION

At the end of 1986 there were two 'schools of excellence', New South Wales and Melbourne, and five Regional Schools:

> Macquarie University
> The Royal Melbourne Institute of Technology
> The University of Queensland
> The University of Adelaide
> The University of Western Australia

Postgraduate degrees were also provided by other Universities and Colleges of Advanced Education. In addition, there were a variety of first degrees, diplomas and certificates offered.

The award of the title Regional School to an institution had not had much practical effect. It did not appear to have affected the institution's funding and those not designated as Regional Schools had not been precluded from providing MBA degrees.

Executive programs were being conducted by various institutions including the New South Wales and Melbourne Schools, the Australian Administrative Staff College and the various divisions of the Australian Institute of Management.

In-house courses had proliferated in number and form. However, it has been noted that, in some organisations, such activities are among the first to suffer from the effects of economies induced by a downturn in economic conditions.

There had been some development in courses in small business management, entrepreneurship and 'intrepreneurship', particularly at Chisholm Institute of Technology in Victoria. However, management education for small business suffers from a lack of clarity as to who would benefit from it, who should provide it and what should be the content.

Consultants had not entered the management education field on a large scale. Perhaps it does not offer sufficient financial rewards over a long period. PA Management Consultants being one of the few such organisations active in the field.

Until the beginning of 1987, the major developments following the Cyert and Ralph Inquiries had been organisational: what sort of structures should be constructed to provide management education? However, during 1987, the form and content of Australian management education was examined more closely. In particular, the traditional, generalist MBA came under scrutiny.

Three trends, which had surfaced before 1987 but which developed during that year, may be noted:

The growth of specialist courses.
The encouragement of 'user-pays'.
The increasing emphasis on research.

Specialisation
There are three ways of providing specialisation:

A program with a compulsory core and a wide choice of electives, such as the MBAs of New South Wales and Monash Universities.

A standardised program with students, on graduation, having the option to continue so as to obtain a further specialised qualification.

A degree or diploma specialising in a certain field, e.g. Public Policy at the Australian National University, Health Services Management at the Royal Melbourne Institute of Technology (RMIT), Organisation Behaviour at Swinburne Institute of Technology.

During 1987, the Royal Melbourne Institute of Technology put a proposal to the Victorian Post-Secondary Education Commission to supplement its

Graduate Diploma in Health Services Management with a Master of Business in the same field. At approximately the same time, Swinburne Institute of Technology proposed supplementing its Graduate Diploma in Organisation Behaviour with a Master of Business in Organisation Behaviour.

Monash University has, since the mid-1960s, offered a Master of Administration (titled changed to Master of Business Administration in 1987) with a wide range of electives. During 1987, it put forward a proposal to introduce a research/coursework degree of Master of Management specialising in any one of the following areas.

> Business Policy
> Business Systems
> Health Administration
> Industrial Relations
> International Business
> Marketing
> Organisational Studies
> Public Sector Management

The Melbourne MBA has, since its inception, been the archetypal generalist Australian postgraduate degree in management, with few, if any, electives. However, the Melbourne Graduate School of Management has commenced to offer candidates for its MBA a greater choice. Beginning in 1988, a candidate in order to qualify for the degree, must complete 20 semester subjects, 13 of which are compulsory and 7, chosen from a list of 12, are electives.

User-Pays

Tertiary education in Australia is free for residents excepting for a small administration fee of $250 per year. An Overseas Student Charge was introduced in 1979, in 1987 the annual fee was A$4660 per student.

Deteriorating economic conditions, the financial problems of the Commonwealth Government, which funds tertiary education, and the acceptance in some quarters of economic-rationalist theories has led to pressure to permit, encourage or force tertiary institutions to charge fees, at least for second-degrees.

So far, the introduction of fees for residents has been resisted by a strong section of the Australian Labor Party, the party which is in office in the Commonwealth. However, a number of tertiary institutions are experimenting with various forms of user-pays. Beginning in 1985, they have been permitted to charge fees to overseas students. The Melbourne Graduate School of Management, in 1987, introduced a one-year Postgraduate Diploma in Management Studies for fee-paying overseas students. The University of Sydney and Macquarie University commenced, in 1988, to offer MBA degrees to such students.

The Graduate School of Management in the University of Melbourne introduced an Executive MBA in 1988. This is a general, one-year management program for students, resident or non-resident sponsored by organisations. Initially the student spends three weeks in residence. This is followed by twenty-two residential weekends and concludes with a residential period of two weeks. The fee charged, covering tuition, library and computer facilities and meals and accommodation is A$22,000.

In an article in The Sydney Morning Herald of 5th November 1987 entitled 'Scholarly battle for the private dollar', David McKnight outlined some of the fee-charging programs 'used as money-spinners for financially-strapped campuses'.

Geoff Maslen, in the Melbourne Age of 4th December 1987, in an article entitled 'Education: new growth industry', developed the theme further.

> 'Australia's higher education institutions are making an astonishing effort to attract thousands of foreign students to study here. Backed by the Federal Government, the institutions have sent teams of academic salesmen into Asian countries in recent months to recruit as many full-fee-paying prospects as they can find'.

This tendency, of course, is evident with regard to tertiary courses in areas other than management.

Research
Comparatively little attention was paid to research in the early Australian 'Business Schools', a fact noted in both the Cyert and Ralph Inquiries. The major task was to build-up the skills, in terms of students, staff and facilities, not to expand the frontiers of academic knowledge. Few of the early staff possessed doctorates, although most had a fair amount of managerial experience; few published, they received little encouragement to do so. There were not many Ph.D. candidates and those who did engage in doctoral studies chose 'practical'

rather than 'theoretical' subjects for their research. The first three candidates to complete the Ph.D. at the Melbourne Graduate School of Business Administration chose as their subjects the problems of small business, the administration of the University of Melbourne and the management of research laboratories.

Today, the possession of a Ph.D. is mandatory in many Australian tertiary management schools in order to obtain an academic appointment. The typical young academic in an Australian 'business school' possesses a Ph.D. but little experience in management. Ph.D. candidates are encouraged. Staff are expected to 'publish or perish'. Some of the research topics appear to be of a somewhat esoteric nature.

Despite the increased interest in research there is little evidence that the boundaries of knowledge have been pushed far. Australia still awaits its Simon, Drucker, Woodward, Trist. Some Australian textbooks have been written but the present trend seems to be towards 'Australianising' American books.

Ironically, the greater interest in research has come at a time when, according to a report in the Melbourne Age of 4 December 1987 (James Button: 'Academics may be put to the test',) the Commonwealth Government is considering a proposal which would split the roles of teaching and research in Universities. If this proposal were adopted, an academic would, presumably, be expected to specialise in either teaching or research - not necessarily in both.

The Australian management education scene today appears to be characterised by a mixture of growth, uncertainty and opportunism.

NOTES

1.   Geoffrey Blainey, The Tyranny of Distance,
Sun Books, Melbourne (1966).
2.   N.F.   Hall,   The   Making   of   Higher
Executives: The   Modern   Challenges,   New   York
University   School   of   Commerce,   Accountants   and
Finance, New York (1958), p.59.
3.   Report of the Committee of Inquiry into
Post-Graduate Education for Management, (The Cyert
Report),   Australian   Government   Publishing
Services, Canberra (1970), p.1.
4.   W.J.   Byrt,   'From   Cyert   to   Ralph: Two
Enquiries into Management Education in Australia',
The   Australian   Accountant,   Vol.   52,   No.   11,
(December 1982), pp. 686-687.
5.   Melbourne   University   Business   School
Association, Special Anniversary Issue: The MBA
Programme's First 21 Years (September 1985), p.11.
6.   Philip   Brown,   'Educating   Tomorrow's
Managers   -   How   Will   the   AGSM   Help',   Forum   of
Discussion   and   Debate,   AIESEC   Australia,   (1
September 1976).
7.   Inquiry Into Management Education Report
(the Ralph Report), Canberra (April 1982), p.2.

Chapter Five

MANAGEMENT EDUCATION IN CANADA
John D Blake

THE CANADIAN ECONOMY

Canada is the world's second largest nation, with
an area of almost ten million square kilometres.
With a population of just over 25 million Canada is
also one of the world's richest nations, although
Gross National Product (GNP) per capita is dropping
relative to the rest of the world - from 3rd place
in 1970 to 11th place in 1982.(1)
      Such a huge country naturally offers a range of
environments. Most of the population is scattered
along the southern border. In Eastern Canada the St
Lawrence valley and the Great Lakes traditionally
provided good routes between regions, but there are
no similar natural transportation routes into
Western Canada.The completion of the Canadian
Pacific Railway's transcontinental line in 1885 was
a deliberate and spectacular piece of nation
building. Nevertheless, many parts of Canada have
easier and more natural lines of communication with
the USA than with the rest of Canada.
      Canada is rich in a wide variety of natural
resources, including fish, forestry, agriculture,
coal, oil, uranium and a variety of minerals
including iron ore. Exploitation of these resources
has created a strong area of industrial activity in
their processing. As an example, Canada's tobacco
industry processes imported as well as locally
grown tobacco. Traditionally, Canada has benefited
from having this wide range of primary products,
since the national economy is thereby protected
against cyclical price movements in individual

products.(2) However, during the 1980s the Canadian economy has suffered from the worldwide trend of a fall in the relative value of primary goods.(3)

Manufacturing industry has been stimulated historically by a high tariff policy, although in recent years tariffs have fallen considerably, particularly with the USA, through international agreement. In particular, US companies sought access to Canadian markets through the establishment of Canadian branch plants. Canada benefited from access to the latest US technology and designs, proven in the world's largest market, as well as US capital. US investment undoubtedly gave Canada fast and relatively easy industrialisation but at costs of which Canadians have become increasingly aware. Safarian(4) lists the main perceived problems of dependence on US owned industry as:

a) The opportunities for Canadians to serve in senior management ranks are limited.
b) Canadian subsidiaries have a limited scope for decision making.
c) There is a tendency for a subsidiary to be limited in its export activities, to avoid competition with the parent company.
d) The subsidiary may be forced to buy parts from the US parent, denying opportunities to local suppliers.
e) Research and Development tends to be centralised in the US.
f) US parent companies are likely to give priority to US rather than Canadian problems.

Safarian's research, involving comparison with similar Canadian-owned businesses, did not in fact find evidence to support all these claimed problems. A more serious problem is that, as the US lead in manufacturing technology has been cut back, Canada has suffered in line. Indeed, one suggested solution has been to seek expanded Japanese investment in Canada.

Canadian industry has a record of relatively low spending on Research and Development, whether owned locally or abroad. Subsidiaries of US-owned companies actually seem to spend more on Research and Development than do Canadian-owned companies, but this spending tends to focus on the adaptation of US technology to local Canadian conditions. Government support is similarly limited. In 1968

Canada's spending on Research and Development, at 1.3 per cent of GNP, was actually lower than the previous year and was some half the levels reached by Japan, West Germany, the US and Sweden.(5)

Canadian manufacturing plants tend to show lower productivity, both in use of labour and capital, than do similar US plants. Traditionally, this has been attributed to US economies of scale. In fact, Daly et al found that average plant sizes were slightly larger in Canada than in the USA.(6) They found that the major problem faced by Canadian plants was that they had to undertake a greater range of products than their US counterparts and so suffered from shorter production runs and more frequent changeovers of production lines.

International competitiveness is of particular importance to Canada as one of the world's leading trading nations. In 1985, Canada was the world's 7th largest exporter with 4.6 per cent of world exports (US $87,500m), and the world's 8th largest importer with 3.8 per cent of world imports. Not surprisingly, Canada's largest trade partner is the USA which, in 1985, took 78 per cent of Canada's total exports.

To summarise, as Canada moves towards the 1990s the country faces three major economic problems:

a) A continuing heavy dependence on the exploitation of natural resources poses problems in a period of generally declining commodity prices.

b) The availability of cheap energy and easy access to natural resources fails to compensate for inefficient production attributable to lack of plant specialisation and this poses a particular danger in an age of increased global competitiveness.

c) A traditional reliance on US technology made available through branch plants means that the relative decline of the USA in technology has a 'knock-on' effect for Canada, which has a record of low investment in Research and Development.

Each of these problems has part of its solution in the education of Canadian managers who need to be more aware of the issues facing primary industries, more flexible in plant management, and more alert to technological innovation.

THE PROVINCIAL STRUCTURE

The provinces of Canada were brought together in the British North America Act, enacted by the United Kingdom parliament in 1867. In practice, the terms of federation were agreed by the provinces between themselves, and a major motive for union was fear of the expansionist ambitions of the USA following the conclusion of the American Civil War.

The ten provinces of Canada can be considered under four broad headings:

a) The Atlantic provinces of Newfoundland, Prince Edward Island, New Brunswick and Nova Scotia, with a total population of some 2,307,500.
The region is heavily dependent on fishing, forestry, farming and mining and the region's population is more rural than the national average.

b) Quebec province, with a population of some 6,582,700, is the main centre for the Francophones, who make up some 80 per cent of the province's population. Traditionally, Quebec has had a strong industrial economy but since the 1960s older industries have tended not to be replaced by the new growth industries, partly as a result of political unrest in the province.

c) Ontario province has a total population of some 9,064,200. Ontario is the manufacturing heartland of Canada, with a rather more modern industrial structure than Quebec and with some 60 per cent of Canada's USA-owned plants.

d) Western Canada embraces the four provinces of Alberta, British Columbia, Manitoba and Saskatchewan, with a total population of some 7,331,100. Although this population averages out at some four persons per square mile, it tends to be concentrated in a few metropolitan centres. The economic base of these provinces varies but, overall, is heavily dependent on agriculture and the exploitation of natural resources.

In addition to these ten provinces, Canada also includes the federally administered North West Territory and the Yukon, vast areas with a total population of some 74,200.

Although, for convenience, we have considered some provinces in groups in this summary, it is important to appreciate that each province has its own elected provincial administration. The British North America Act of 1867 explicitly states 'In and for each Province the Legislature may exclusively make laws in relation to Education' (S93). Thus, not only does each province have its own industrial structure but also its own system of education, including higher education. The federal government needs to tread with great care in attempting to formulate any kind of national policy relating to higher education for fear of offending provincial governments. As an example, when the Canadian government set up a system of supporting the education of veterans of World War II, this was described as 'university training' rather than 'university education' in order to avoid any suggestion that the federal government was trespassing on the provinces' monopoly of education.(7)

CANADA AND THE 'THIRD WORLD'

Although Canada is, as we have seen, one of the wealthiest countries in the world, there are certain aspects of Canada's position which help promote some affinity with the 'third world'. Canada is heavily dependent on the export of natural resources and is a major importer of manufactured goods. Moreover, a high proportion of Canadian natural resources and industry are owned and controlled outside Canada's borders. Thus, Canada is regarded by some as 'the world's wealthiest developing country'.(8)

This identification with the third world is reinforced by Canada's active participation in the United Nations, the British Commonwealth and the Francophone community. Canada has traditionally maintained more friendly relations with left-wing governments in Latin America, including Cuba, than has the USA.

Thus, Canada is especially well placed to act as an intermediary between the developed countries and the third world.

This relationship has been strengthened by personal ties. The British Commonwealth first established a secretariat in 1965 and the first head, Mr Arnold Smith, was a Canadian. In 1970, French-speaking countries established their own agency, ACCT, and, again, the first head of the secretariat, Mr Jean-Marc Leger, was a Canadian. As a consequence, strong fraternal relationships between the two organisations have developed. In 1987, when both organisations happened to meet in Canada, half the world's nations were represented. (Reported in The Economist 2 August 1987, p 57).

To take another example, the four Atlantic provinces have formed an Association of Atlantic Universities. The University of the West Indies has chosen to establish links with this Association rather than, as might be expected, some form of US association.(9)

This strong 'third world' link represents a substantial opportunity both for business and universities in Canada.

HIGHER EDUCATION FOR MANAGEMENT

In 1986, Canada had a total of 68 universities, as shown in Table 5.1. Some of these are very small institutions, with as few as a hundred students. This relatively (for Canada's population) large number of universities is due to four factors:

a) Many of the smaller universities have been founded by particular religious denominations.
b) Because of Canada's large land mass it is necessary to spread around a large number of small institutions to ensure that most of the population have easy access to a university.
c) Each province has control of its own higher education system. Thus, some elements of duplication in provision is unavoidable.
d) Those provinces with substantial numbers of both French and English speakers tend to have separate French-speaking and English-speaking universities.

Rapid growth of the Canadian higher education system since World War II, particularly in the 1960s, resulted in a demand for academic staff that could not be met within Canada. At the key stage of expansion of the system, the pattern of development was dominated by foreign nationals. For example, in 1971 the University of Calgary reported the following make-up of their academic staff:(10)

```
              Canadians          405
              USA                196
              UK                 149
              India/Pakistan      33
              Other               34
```

Table 5.1: Canadian universities as at 1986

	Under-graduate only	Under-graduate & masters	Under-graduate masters & doctoral
Newfoundland			1
Prince Edward Island	1		
Nova Scotia	4	6	2
New Brunswick	1	2	1
Quebec	1	1	6
Ontario	2	7	12
Manitoba	3	2	1
Saskatchewan	1	-	2
Alberta	1	2	2
British Columbia	2	2	3
Total	16	22	30

Source: 'Education in Canada - a statistical
        review for 1985-86', Statistics Canada.

This influx of foreign nationals facilitated rapid
expansion and, indeed, was supported by Government
tax incentives. However, Canadian academics became
aware of a danger of foreign domination and a
national symposium of Canadian universities in May
1971 went so far as to pass a resolution calling on
the federal government to limit the number of
foreign nationals teaching at Canadian universities. In fact, during the 1970s, university expansion moved to higher degree programs and Canadian
higher education now produces an ample supply of
well-qualified candidates for academic posts, many
of whom find academic employment abroad as well as
in Canada.

Canadian universities offer a wide range of
business programs. Table 5.2 shows how enrolments
both in business subjects and on all undergraduate
programs have grown during the 1980s.

Table 5.2: Undergraduate enrolments 1981/1986

In business subjects:

	Male	Female	Total
1981/82	28,829	17,084	45,913
1982/83	29,204	18,642	47,846
1983/84	28,729	20,106	48,835
1984/85	27,973	20,535	48,508
1985/86	28,144	21,399	49,543

In Total:

1981/82	189,226	165,521	354,747
1982/83	200,130	176,084	374,747
1983/84	209,003	188,348	397,351
1984/85	210,586	195,720	406,306
1985/86	210,806	201,628	412,434

Rush and Evers[11] report the results of a survey which considered how Canadian university graduates and corporate employers viewed the adequacy of university education compared with the human resource requirements of Canadian corporations. Overall they found 'reasonable satisfaction' with the higher education system. Criticism of the system was principally concerned with complaints that undergraduate courses had been too technical in content, failing to cultivate communication and personal skills. Business graduates were least satisfied with the creative and innovative skills they had developed. A typical complaint read:

'University does not properly initiate leadership or administrative skills. There is far too much emphasis on developing quantitative skills and virtually no emphasis on administrative or organisa-tional skills. In the commerce program, no effort is really made to develop one's communication skills.'

In addition to the university sector, Canada has an extensive range of post secondary-education institutions known as 'community colleges'. These offer a range of two year courses in both academic and technical streams, as well as further programs for adults. They offer students a shorter route to work than do universities, but with a chance to enter a university course if they choose, with credit for work covered at the college. An OECD Report identified the community colleges as 'the

most attractive educational achievement made in
Canada' offering a flexible approach to the
educational needs of all age groups.(12) In 1985/86
some 65,000 students were enrolled in business and
commercial courses in Canadian community colleges.

Funding for higher education has not kept up
with student demand. Between 1977/78 and 1984/85
the number of students in universities increased by
27 per cent and in community colleges by 36 per
cent. However, adjusted for inflation, the total of
federal and provincial outlays increased by only
2.5 per cent. Because of the provincial structure,
this government funding is spread fairly evenly
over the universities, while fee structures are
fixed so that it is not practical for generously-
resourced centres of excellence to emerge. No
Canadian university has repeated the pattern found
in the most prestigious US institutions, with large
graduate programs and relatively small undergraduate activity. Where staff/student ratios in
leading US universities tend to fall in the range
of 1:7 to 1:12, in Canada the range is 1:18 to
1:24.

MBA programs are well established in Canada,
currently running in 28 universities and producing
some 2,200 graduates a year - more than double the
output of MBA's per head of population in the UK;
though way behind the USA. Canadian industry seems
satisfied with Canada's MBA's, although the
Canadian Manufacturers' Association has called for
a strengthening of the business schools' international marketing programs.

Many Canadian students find the most prestigious US business schools more attractive than
Canada's. A study of 44 Canadian students on the
Harvard MBA program (reported in the 'Globe &
Mail', 23 March 1987) found that they had faced
intense competition for their places and accepted
heavy financial sacrifices to go on the course.
Some 40 per cent planned to stay in the USA,
generally quoting better financial prospects to
explain this decision. By contrast, those planning
to return to Canada tended to cite more idealistic
grounds, talking of making a contribution to the
improvement of Canada's industry. A quote from one
student, 'A Harvard degree carries more weight in
Toronto than a Western degree' (i.e. one from the
University of Western Ontario) summed up the
feeling that Canada's business schools cannot match
the achievements of the USA's best.

CORPORATE MANAGEMENT DEVELOPMENT

In the period 1985 to 1986 the Banff Centre School of Management conducted a national survey of business views on management training in Canada.(13) The survey covered senior executives in large organisations in the primary sector, secondary industries, the services sector and the public sector.

The survey found that most organisations have some form of executive development committee, composed of senior vice-presidents, to lay down the basic philosophy for executive development. Desired outcomes at this level tend to be expressed in the most general terms along the lines of 'broadening the individual', 'facilitating growth' and 'becoming aware of other thought processes'.

At the implementation level more specific objectives tend to be discussed but even then these tend to be expressed in very general terms. Examples quoted in the survey include 'to look at oneself and the organisation', 'to stand back', 'to work in abstract' and 'to acquire confidence'.

Most companies in the survey accepted that their executive development programs did not involve any rigorous process of identifying and matching the needs of the individual and the organisation. Generally, a request to attend a particular management development program comes from the individual employee rather than the employer.

Most companies accepted that this approach to management development was an area of weakness and some of the smaller companies had recently engaged in more sophisticated in-depth analysis of their management development needs. In some cases, consultants had been employed to interview employees and identify needs.

Generally, the outcome of management programs is not systematically evaluated. Feedback is generally subjective and informal in nature. It is unusual for career progression of employees to be checked out against the management development programs they have undertaken, in order to consider the effectiveness of the programs.

The Banff study found the ten major areas of perceived needs in management development were, in order:

a) Communicative systems and skills. This area covered planning and reporting systems and skills in basic oral and written communication, negotiation with employees, customer relations, media handling and presentational skills.

b) Creative, transformational or inspirational leadership. In particular, chief executives wanted senior managers to develop the skills to motivate staff who are likely to see their organisations become more 'lean and mean' over the years.

c) Management development, embracing both the ability to function as a manager and a range of specific business skills.

d) Management of change, seen as the ability to respond to new opportunities and cope with the challenge of rapidly changing conditions.

e) Strategic planning and management.

f) Business - Government relations, an area where private sector managers seemed much more concerned than those from the public sector.

g) Management of technology, focusing on the information revolution.

h) Marketing strategy.

i) Organisational effectiveness.

j) 'The basics',embracing planning, prioritising, problem-solving and inter-personal skills.

Not surprisingly, this list shows a concern to develop the manager's approach to people and the organisation rather than to implant specific skills and knowledge.

Generally, Canadian business prefers to send managers on externally-run courses, mainly at the university business schools, rather than 'in-house' courses. Business schools are judged on their ability to produce an intensive, interactive environment rather than on technical program content.

This brings us to what is, in practice, one of the main functions of Canadian management development. Canadian managers are drawn from across a large country, from a relatively large number of universities, many of them small. Because of the provincial structure, there is not the concentration of excellence in a small number of higher education institutions found in many other countries. Thus, there is not opportunity for potential high-flying managers to build up a network of personal contacts before entering business. The management development programs run at the business schools bring together managers from a wide range of organisations and so facilitate the construction

of a network of contacts. In evaluating the importance of such programs one executive suggests that
success is 70 per cent attributable to participant
mix and only 30 per cent to program content. Thus,
a distinctive role of the Canadian management
development industry is the construction of an 'old
boy' system.

MANAGEMENT EDUCATION AND THE DEVELOPING COUNTRIES

A major strength of the Canadian business schools
is derived from Canada's strong links with the
developing world. The Canadian International
Development Agency has given financial support to a
number of projects where Canadian business schools
run executive management programs in the developing
countries. These are designed to reflect local
priorities. As an example, a two-week program run
in Kenya by the University of Western Ontario
emphasises:

'A unique feature of the course is the use
of on-site cases and local materials. These
are integrated and contrasted with international situations in other countries'.
(Reported 'Business Quarterly' November
1986, p.7.)

Another example of the support given to international management development by the Canadian
International Development Agency has been the
sponsoring of two seminars, one in Canada and one
in the Philippines, where managers and business
academics from Canada and various Asian countries
were brought together. These seminars identified a
number of areas where the Asian business environment differs from that in the west including:

a) The Asian manager has a deep sense of family
    and community, and is sensitive to the socio-
    cultural systems imposed by western-based
    management approaches.
b) The Asian manager is less aggressive than the
    western manager, approaching problems with a
    degree of patience and being inclined to allow
    solutions to emerge over a period of time.
c) Asia has a larger proportion of local small
    family-owned businesses. The few large Asian
    businesses tend to adopt a more western style
    of management approach.

d) Where the traditional western approach to management education focuses on large urban based business, in many of the developing countries of Asia the rural sector represents some 80 per cent of the population.

e) Asian business tends to value an employee for loyalty as much as for achievement.

f) Asian business schools find the 'publish or perish' syndrome common in western business schools unattractive, tending to lead to research designed for prestige publications rather than broader social objectives.(14)

This willingness of the Canadian business and academic community to assess differences in the business environment of the developing countries equips the Canadian business schools both to prepare their own students for international management and to provide management education for the developing countries. The Canadian business schools offer a pleasing contrast to the USA, where students from developing countries find both staff and fellow students unsympathetic to their special interests.

However, a lack of awareness of the impact of local conditions on the type of management education required in a country is not confined to the west. The author was told by a leading Canadian academic specialising in finance of how a university in one developing country asked him to run a program for managers. When he raised the question of using local case material he was told that the university was not interested in this - they wanted the most up-to-date western theory, irrespective of its relevance to local conditions.

Overall, Canada's strong links with the developing world, combined with a receptive approach by the Canadian academic community, have made the Canadian business schools an attractive proposition for the management development needs of third world countries.

MANAGEMENT EDUCATION AND WOMEN

The proportion of women amongst managers and aspirant managers in Canada has, as in most parts of the western world, been increasing. From 1970 to 1980 the proportion of women in management and administrative roles increased from 13 per cent to 21 per cent while women's wages as a percentage of men's in such roles increased from 51 per cent to 60 per cent.(15)

During the 1980s undergraduate enrolments in business subjects have changed as follows:

	Per cent of total male	Per cent of total female
1981/82	63	37
1982/83	61	39
1983/84	59	41
1984/85	58	42
1985/86	57	43

Over this period, male enrolments in business subjects fell by some 700 while female enrolments rose by some 4,300. Thus, the increased number of women aspiring to business careers is compensating for a drop in male entrants and also providing growth. The Canadian Manufacturers' Association is aware of the importance of recruiting women to management positions and has recommended 'the involvement of women students in science, engineering and business programs should be increased substantially'.(16)

However, there is evidence to suggest that women face considerable problems in the pursuit of equal work opportunities. Canadian census data show that in answer to the question 'Do women in Canada get as good a break as men?' the number of people replying 'yes' dropped from 64 per cent in 1971 to 47 per cent in 1983. Similarly, in answering the question 'Do able women have as good a chance as able men to become executives?' in both 1970 and 1980 the same proportion of respondents, 42 per cent answered 'yes'.

A research study by faculty at the University of Western Ontario looked at two groups of MBAs who had graduated in the years 1976 to 1982, ten men and ten women from each year. The study shows very different levels of perceived attainment:

Level of Management	Women Per cent	Men Per cent
Low	39	11
Middle	48	53
Senior	5	26
Entrepreneur	7	10

These different levels of attainment can be explained in part by the family pressures on women. The research study looked at how respondents felt their priorities had changed since graduation. Forty-four per cent of married women felt they now regarded their families as more important, compared with only 30 per cent of married men. Conversely, 54 per cent of married men regarded their business careers as becoming more important, compared with 22 per cent of married women.

The survey also identified ways in which management development programs could give more support to women managers. It found that a number of women felt that they received less effective feedback on job performance than men and also tended to be sent on different training courses, usually shorter and with different content than those for male managers. As an example of apparent discrimination in the attitudes of those responsible for management training, in 1985 one of Canada's major programs on marketing management had only eight women participants out of a total of 123.

The study also suggests that women suffer in management careers because the career progress towards senior management tends, at higher levels, to depend on skills in the manipulation of organisational politics rather than on technical competence. It is argued that women traditionally have more difficulty than men in this type of manipulation. The suggested remedy is that both men and women managers should be sent on courses geared to helping progress through the organisation.

To summarise, if Canadian business is to make the best use of the resource of women managers it will be necessary both to eliminate discrimination in training and to review the content of management development programs. With the increased proportion of women in management, such a change is as much a commercial necessity as a matter of justice.

CONCLUSION

Canada has a strong record in management education, with a great deal to offer the developing countries. However, the provincial control of Higher Education has prevented the emergence of adequately-resourced centres of excellence capable of matching the achievements of the strongest US business schools.

NOTES

1.   A.   Blackbourn   &   R.G.   Putnam,   The
Industrial Geography of Canada, Croom Helm, 1984.
2.   D.F.   Walker,   Canada's   Industrial   Space
Economy, Bell & Hyman, 1980.
3.   D.G. Vice, 'Higher Education: The Key to
Competitiveness', Business Quarterly, Summer 1987,
pp. 85-90.
4.   A.E. Safarian, The performance of foreign
owned firms in Canada, Canadian-American Committee,
1969.
5.   D.G. Vice, 'Higher Education: The Key to
Competitiveness'.
6.   D.J. Daly, et al, Scale and Specialisation
in Canadian Manufacturing, Economic Council of
Canada, 1968.
7.   E. Sheffield, 'The National Scene', in
Sheffield et al, Systems of Higher Education:
Canada, ICED, 1978.
8.   J.   O'Manique,   'The   response   of   the
principal sectors of Canadian society to the NIEO',
in E. Laszlo & J. Kurtzman, The United States,
Canada, and the New International Economic Order,
Pergamon, 1979.
9.   J. Holmes, 'The Atlantic Provinces', in
Sheffield et al, Systems of Higher Education:
Canada, ICED, 1978.
10.   J. Katz, Education in Canada, David &
Charles, 1974.
11.   J.C. Rush & F.T. Evers, 'Making the match:
Canada's   university   graduates   and   corporate
employers', Business Quarterly, Summer 1987, pp.
85-90.
12.   OECD, Reviews of National Policies for
Education - Canada, OECD, 1976.
13.   D.G. Vice, 'Higher Education: The Key to
Competitiveness'.
14.   P.M.   Maher   &   A.   Gupta,   'The   role   of
Canadian management schools in training managers
for Asia', Business Quarterly, Summer 1986, pp.
48-51.
15.   D.M. Mikalachki & A. Mikalachki, 'Women in
Business - Going for Broke', Business Quarterly,
Summer 1985, pp. 25-32.
16.   D.G. Vice, 'Higher Education: The Key to
Competitiveness'.

Chapter Six

MANAGEMENT EDUCATION IN FRANCE
Jean-Louis Barsoux

Management education is not a single-track along
which countries are well or badly positioned. It is
a series of parallel tracks. Different countries
train managers at different levels for different
purposes. The scope and emphasis of any system are
products of a unique historical configuration. They
are shaped by a country's economy, its management
structure, its educational, social and cultural
traditions and, most importantly, by its receptiveness to American influence.

To understand the present state of French
management education it is important to retrace its
evolution which has its roots in the engineering
grandes écoles. These have long been the favoured
avenue into management.

AN HISTORICAL SKETCH

Conventional wisdom has it that France has been a
late developer in the field of management
education. Yet it can be argued that France played
a pioneering role when the state set up a number of
prestigious grandes écoles at the turn of the
eighteenth century. The alumni of these engineering
schools were groomed (and still are) to take up
positions as les cadres de la nation, in spheres as
diverse as business, politics and public service.
In fact, the schools' legitimacy as suppliers of
the nation's business elite does not rest on the
curriculum (albeit generalist in content) but on
the type of education. Form outweighs substance.

120

The seal of approval from a top engineering school endorses its holder's capacity for rapid learning and intellectual virtuosity. The quality of the raw material is guaranteed by a highly selective recruitment process, which requires two years additional schooling after the end of secondary education - and the finished product has the added feature of three years of intensive study. In short, the graduate engineer is endowed with the necessary resolve and analytical ability to tackle any problem.

Moreover, by virtue of this early pooling of versatile talent, the future leaders are able to establish links which will serve them throughout their careers. Influential networks are constituted even before entering the fray of the business world. This is particularly important in view of the way the state has impinged upon the private sector and the consequent need for dialogue. The social cohesion born of a common education and, by implication, social background, has also eased mid-career transfers from the public to the private sector - a one-way flow known as _pantouflage_ (discussed later).

There are also repercussions on behaviour. Preconditioned into believing that they are bound for the boardroom, the would-be leaders start to act accordingly. Anticipatory socialisation ensures that they acquire the poise and outlook of leadership. This belief is merely reinforced by firms which are eager to give these high-flyers preferential career advancements, thereby establishing an artificial track record and legitimising their leadership positions.

The type of education inculcated in these _grandes écoles,_ has implications for the way senior management posts are filled. On graduating, a _polytechnicien_(1), for instance, has assembled a battery of real or assumed advantages that ensure speedy ascent. Indeed, the success of engineering schools in promoting themselves as 'surrogate management schools' partly explains the belated emergence of American-style business schools in France.

For nearly a century, the engineering schools had it all their own way. Certainly they were not threatened by the inception of the first commercial school, later to become the Ecole Supérieur de Commerce de Paris (ESCP)(2), set up by the Chamber of Commerce and Industry of Paris (CCIP) in 1819. Nor were they initially worried by the CCIP's subsequent attempt to challenge their dominance by creating the Ecole des Hautes Etudes Commerciales (HEC) in 1881.

This school was set up, amid indifference towards commerce, with the express intention of breaking the engineers' stranglehold over large sectors of business in the expanding industrial climate of the late nineteenth century. From the outset, HEC imitated what were considered the most prestigious aspects of the state-sponsored engineering schools - notably a socially biased, post-baccalauréat recruitment policy. Furthermore, HEC's curriculum rested firmly on the cornerstone of law, a noble discipline which lent commercial education a veneer of academic respectability. In terms of image, it looked to the Ecole Centrale for guidance since this was the only private engineering school which had managed to stamp its identity among the state grandes écoles (the very first HEC Directeur was a Centralien).

The latter part of the nineteenth century saw a number of regional Chambers of Commerce follow the Parisian lead. However, the schools they set up were fairly parochial in outlook, catering for and recruiting from the surrounding market. The sons of local businessmen were fed a staple diet of law and accountancy which was no match for the high-powered curricula of the engineering schools.

By 1900 there were ten regional commercial schools which would later form the core of the ESCAE(3) network (today's commercial grandes écoles). These had nothing to do with the universities since the latter were not noted for the practical application of their teaching or research. So, as in the field of engineering, commerce set up its own establishments, thereby widening the gulf between the professionally-oriented form of education in the grandes écoles and the classical focus of the universities and giving rise to France's distinctive two-tier higher education system.

The thinking of Taylor, and to a lesser extent Fayol, spawned a number of discussion groups in the 1920s. Some of these evolved into embryonic management development centres in the 1930s. These were the first establishments to provide a semblance of what might be termed business education. Strictly speaking then, French management education was launched with post-experience students in non-university settings. Of these centres and institutes educating adults, the most notable was the CEGOS(4) which catered for practising managers but only became really active in courses and seminars after World War II and which reigned supreme in France until the large American consultancy firms arrived on the scene in the 1960s.

It was not until 1929 that the American managerial lead was explicitly acknowledged by an observation mission to the US. The CCIP sent a small group of people to the universities of Harvard, New York, Chicago, Columbia and North Western. They returned with a welter of observations which were at the base of the foundation of the Centre de Perfectionnement aux Affaires (CPA) in 1930 by the CCIP. This was the first senior management training centre in Europe and, by its immediate adoption of the case study method, demonstrated France's early receptiveness to US methods.

The post-war economic reconstruction saw a quantum leap in the development of management education. The French Chambers of Commerce were particularly active in promoting exchanges by businessmen, senior civil servants and teachers to the US to study business organisation and management methods. Story and Parrott refer to 'streams of French businessmen' who headed for the US to prostrate themselves before sales guru, Jose Trujillo.(5)

Until the mid-50s French management education was spearheaded by the efforts of the Chambers of Commerce with the CCIP leading the charge. In 1954, however, the French Employers Federation (CNPF) contributed to the drive by creating the Centre de Recherche et d'Etudes des Chefs d'Entreprise (CRC), designed to initiate senior executives to modern managerial methods. Its softer approach was in stark contrast to the preceding preoccupation with the rationalisation of manual work and the narrowly technical conception of the organisation which had been preached by management consultants with engineering backgrounds (mostly Centraliens). It marked a shift from organisation education to management education.

Likewise, the state's interest was only aroused in the mid-50s when a promising market already existed. It made a belated entrance, through the dual channels of the universities and the Institut de Controle de Gestion (since renamed Institut Français de Gestion). The latter, created in 1956, was again the fruit of a productivity mission to the US, this time by a study group from the Planning Commission. It offered managers a practical grounding in management techniques.

123

As for the universities, in 1955, they finally overcame their longstanding aversion to all things managerial. Until then, no state institutions of higher education had offered management courses per se, considering them unworthy of academic attention. Five Institut d'Administration des Entreprises (IAE) were set up within universities to teach one year post-graduate diplomas. There are now 18 IAEs but their standing is tarnished by the university image in relation to the 'voie royale' offered by the grandes écoles. The status differences can be gauged from the disparate salaries offered.

In business circles, there was a growing awareness of the French managerial lag which provoked the alumni association of the Ecole des Hautes Etudes Commerciales (HEC) to recommend a change in the curriculum in 1952. A reform was eventually forthcoming in 1958. This signalled a transition from commercial schools to écoles de gestion, specifically inspired by the American model - a shift symbolised by the rediscovery of the case study method(6) and the move away from lecture-theatre pedagogy. This was a vital turning point in the evolution of French management education. The American model did not generate clones but grafted itself upon the existing infrastructure of grandes écoles which helps to explain the uniqueness of the French system. Following the cue of HEC, the other commercial schools gradually revised their curricula, making room for the new disciplines by cutting down on the law and accountancy inputs.

Further corroboration of the perceived US advance lay in the pilgrimage west, this time for personal motives rather than state-inspired, by the cream of the commercial and engineering schools, in order to round off their education with an MBA. France seemed quite infatuated with American management and was, in fact, the European nation which dispatched the largest contingents to American business schools. The demand was such that a US-style MBA was created in France to satisfy it.

INSEAD was founded in 1958 on the Harvard model. It drew on American expertise in developing both curriculum and suitable teachers and was sponsored by a group of businessmen belonging to the Paris Chamber of Commerce (CCIP) together with the European Productivity Agency, the body set up to administer Marshall Aid. Its founders were intent on closing the transatlantic management gap but they were staunchly European in outlook. So, the institute was more than a panacea for particular French ailments. It had the more visionary mission of creating a new wave of international managers to coincide with the newly established European Economic Community - hence its three-language curriculum.

The majority of private establishments emerged only when the economic boom of the 60s guaranteed success. There was a notable upsurge in the number of private schools and, with high enrolment fees, a business school could prove a highly profitable business. This perhaps explains the current pre-occupation with foundation dates. Certain schools of lesser repute are keen to publicise their 60s foundation as a means of disassociating themselves from the bandwagon effect and vaunting their respectability.

The post-war explosion in the number of cadres(7) brought with it a new professional class with its own identity and values. Business education gained unprecedented legitimacy and generated a flourishing industry in business journals with a captive readership. The torch-bearers of the French management press were first l'Express and later l'Expansion, both inspired by the American journal Fortune. They marked the transition of the economic press from one providing financial information for investors to one aimed at encouraging a new business-literate generation of managers. Once again they confirmed the pervasive influence of America on the evolution of French managerial values.

State involvement intensified in 1966, when the government set up Institutes of Technology (IUT) in the universities. These establishments offered two-year management courses for higher technicians and were intended to redress the alleged dearth of middle managers, as well as to attenuate criticism of elitism.

However, this must be considered a hollow boast. The abstract logic traditions of their faculty surroundings were almost calculated to undermine, in the eyes of the employers, IUT claims of practice-centred management education.

The state was spurred on to greater things by the combined stimulants of the 1968 student riots, which questioned the role of the universities, and the publication of Jean-Jacques Servan-Schreiber's provocative work, The American Challenge, which equated France's poor productivity with a manage-rial lag. The state responded by creating the first management university in the recently vacated NATO headquarters. The University Dauphine, had the same inauspicious reception as greeted the fledgling HEC, and was forced to renounce its university origins in order to gain credibility vis-a-vis employers. Thus, it has taken on many of the accoutrements of grande école education, as regards length and format of studies, but more importantly in terms of recruitment. French universities should practise an open-door policy, making any holder of the baccalauréat eligible for admission. However, in the case of Dauphine, the government turns a convenient blind eye in order to uphold the reputation of this jewel in its crown.

Another significant landmark of 1968 was the creation of the National Foundation for Management Education (FNEGE) by the Employers' Federation (CNPF), the Chambers of Commerce and Industry (CCIs) and the Government. In keeping with the tradition of l'Ecole Polytechnique, l'ENA(8) and, most recently, l'Ecole Nationale de l'Exportation, the first impulse had been to create a specialist school to cope with a specific problem. An elite managerial school had been suggested by the creator of l'ENA, Michael Debré, but the idea failed to get enough support. It was shelved and a co-ordinating body, the FNEGE, formed instead.

The state of affairs by the end of the 1960s was an unhappy one; French research in management was negligible and there were few genuine management teachers (other than converted economists or law specialists). So the FNEGE quickly set about its most urgent task, that of training staff. A core of young teachers was sent to America to be trained on doctoral courses and MBAs. This drive lasted from 1970-76 during which time 600 management teachers were trained. The FNEGE then took over and set up doctoral programs in France(9) (six in universities and two in grandes écoles) to ensure a continued supply of management teachers. Unfortunately, the consequences of a skewed age pyramid were not foreseen. The bottleneck of teachers, now aged between 40 and 45, has left impoverished career prospects for anyone wishing to enter the field. As a result, management education is a poor choice of career and most of the places on the doctoral programs are filled by foreign students.

The state's next initiative was to instigate a levy which required firms with more than ten employees to spend at least 1.1 per cent of the payroll on training of workers and managers alike. Companies were forced to pay more attention to training since they were required to draw up a training plan to be submitted to and discussed with the comité d'entreprise (works committee). If a company falls short of the statutory requirement, the balance is forfeited to the Treasury. For this reason, the levy was initially perceived as an extension of the tax burden. But, gradually, firms are starting to look upon it as an investment which can be integrated into the firm's strategy. Needless to say, this legislation, passed in 1971, provoked an immediate rash of consultancy firms hoping to cash-in on obligatory spending.

The first genuine signs of innovation in French management education also appeared throughout the 70s. Six large French firms pooled resources and in association with INSEAD founded a private manage- ment education centre (CEDEP) exclusively for their own personnel. The centre is aimed at developing a critical mass of senior managers within each company who will be imbued with the same values. In 1973, CCIP created the Ecole Européene des Affaires (EAP), a business school whose students spend successive years in Oxford, Paris and Berlin. In 1975, ESSEC, HEC's main rival, conceived 'junior- entreprise', a movement which has since become widespread among business schools, whereby students offer their services, for a fee, to local businesses. In 1978, an agreement was passed between the employers' federation (CNPF) and the unions whereby cadres could be released for up to a year for training purposes (congé formation).

The 80s have brought with them the cult of managerialism and France has embraced the new management gurus with the same enthusiasm with which it greeted sales guru, Jose Trujillo, in the 1950s. Tom Peters' books have sold better in France then anywhere else in Europe and home-grown repli- cas of the books abound. Educating managers through reading has become big business and this has been reinforced by a resurgence of business journals which are helping to disseminate the managerial ethos. What is more, the creation of business schools gives no indication of levelling out. These developments are signs of an unsatisfied appetite for management education. They also point to the belated emergence of an enterprise culture, in a society which has traditionally been hostile to business and profit. France has undergone a radical change in culture and nowhere is this turn around more apparent than in the attitudes of students. In 1968, they were busy trying to burn down the Bourse; today, every self-respecting business school has its own investment club. There is a greater willingness to treat business as socially acceptable and essential to the life of the country.

CURRENT PROVISION FOR MANAGEMENT EDUCATION

Pre-Experience Level

Effectively, management education begins when pupils choose their baccalauréat options. Although there is a gestion option, pupils with real managerial aspirations will steer clear of it. They will choose instead the mathematics and physical sciences option (the notorious bac C) which affords the best chances of successful entry (concours permitting), two years after baccalauréat, into both engineering and commercial grandes écoles. The irony that the management option leads to anything but a high-powered managerial position is compounded by the fact that there are over 20 baccalauréat options but only one which opens all the doors. This situation has been condemned as the dictatorship of the bac C.

On completing the baccalauréat, it is accepted that those who can will proceed to the preparatory schools (prépas) to be coached through the entrance exam (concours) to the grandes écoles. Competition to enter the most successful Parisian prépa (Louis-le-Grand) is said to be tougher than the subsequent entry into one of the prestigious trio of management schools, collectively known as les grandes parisiennes. Students are kept informed of relative success rates of the various prépas by annual 'hit parades' published by the journals l'Etudiant and Le Monde de l'Education, thereby instilling an early notion of career strategy.

Once admitted, the students are subjected to an intense work rate, based essentially on mathematics, which can make the subsequent pace at the grande école seem decidedly slack. For most, this is the peak effort, since once inside a grande école the likelihood of failure is very slim. In fact, the high pressure experienced during this training period prompted The Guardian to dub preparatory schooling, le Cram de la Créme.

Those unable to enter a prépa may opt for a one year Chamber of Commerce and Industry (CCI) course or may choose to enrol at the increasingly rated Instituts Universitaires de Technologie. There are currently 67 of these IUTs and they cater for some 60,000 students. Their mini-concours has turned them into small scale grandes écoles. They offer two year management courses which are vocational in nature. Their reputations are rising as witnessed by shortening lead-times for their students in reaching cadre status. Yet, the IUTs remain 'Cinderella' establishments. This makes them a favourite hunting ground for the large retail stores which are themselves snubbed as vendeurs d'aspirateur (sellers of vacuum cleaners) by grandes écoles graduates.

The university system, too, is attempting to become more vocationally relevant, as seen in the latest course offering, the magistères.(10) However, they remain tainted by the universities' reputation for authoritarian, non-interactive teaching, which does not lend itself to the teaching methods used in management education. The traditionalism of the state universities and the past weakness of relationships between industry and the universities have hindered the progress of management education in the universities. As far as many employers are concerned, their products are still synonymous with the teaching profession and the dole queues.

Whilst most universities suffer from the lingering mistrust of companies, there is a notable exception in the management university, Dauphine. Its selection, competition and professionalism give it all the hallmarks of a grande école. It does not practise arm's length selection and, in failing to do so, defies the law. Nor is it overly concerned about appearing a little elitist. In practice, only people with a bac C (mathematics) need apply and 95 per cent of the intake in fact obtained a distinction in their baccalauréat. This is deemed preferable to selection 'par la file d'attente' or 'par la règle de l'autobus' (first come first served). As a result, its reputation among employers is enhanced and its students can expect increasing numbers of unsolicited job offers.

Dauphine also pays the same attention as the grandes écoles to industrial placements - demonstrating full awareness of the importance of these initial contacts between students and companies. In the same vein, Dauphine has followed the example of the grandes écoles and has organised annual job fairs, as well as a yacht race whose teams are composed of students and executives, and which amounts to a floating job fair. The teaching methods too, are reminiscent of the grandes écoles in that they are based on group work rather than lectures. It would seem that any university which seeks to emulate Dauphine's success is destined to follow the same course and shed its university image.

Those not tempted by l'enfer préparationnaire, and those who fail the grandes écoles entrance exam (concours), are eagerly awaited by a host of alternative schools. Most of these are private and set a token entrance examination - meeting entrance requirements has less to do with the examination marks than with parental funds. The schools demand high tuition fees since they do not have the same ability as the grandes écoles to attract financial support from companies' taxe professionelle.(11) These schools also have some difficulty in attracting permanent academic staff and generally resort to a mixture of part-time teachers and visiting staff. That is not to say they do not know how to market themselves. On the contrary, their less prestigious position makes it essential to maintain a high profile. Guaranteed selling points like an international perspective, old boy networks, sporting associations and junior-entreprise (student-run consultancy) invariably feature prominently in their seductive literature.

These schools are invariably known by acronyms whose similarity can prove quite bewildering, even for the initiated. One personnel manager speculated that new commercial schools were named by picking out three of the following at random: 'école institut, supérieur, hautes études, gestion, finance, direction des entreprises, affaires', and translating the result into English if needs be. There is undoubtedly an element of deliberate trompe l'oeil in many appellations - to dupe would-be students, their parents and potential employees alike. But the schools are still being created at a steady rate.

Few of these schools actually have government accreditation. This may range from the basic recognition of the establishment to the more exclusive recognition of its diploma which entails the Ministry of Education having some say in the syllabus and teaching methods as well as naming the Chairman of the Admissions and Examiners' Board. Only 37 schools award a state-recognised diploma. But many more are designated homologué par l'Etat which simply indicates the level of the diploma.

Again the less scrupulous schools play on the popular confusion surrounding the various degrees of state accreditation.

Access to the commercial grandes écoles is via concours. Many of the schools gauge their popularity by the number of times they are over-subscribed and use these figures in their publicity. Oddly enough, it is not necessarily the top schools which attract the most candidates since there is a large measure of self-selection. French students are sensitised early into optimising their chances and cutting their losses, so they will only enter for examinations which they are capable of passing.

The leading three, HEC-ESSEC-ESCP, are closely followed by the regional CCI-sponsored Ecoles Supérieures de Commerce (led by Lyon) mingled with a few of the private schools just mentioned. The level of consensus surrounding the pecking order is high and there is little movement near the top. The ranking is perpetuated by regular comparisons in various journals (notably l'Etudiant, le Monde de l'Education) but is, perhaps, fuelled most by l'Expansions's annual cote des débutants in which explicit comparisons are made using salary offers. The preoccupation with these surveys is extraordinary. One observer of the system was of the opinion that: 'The heads of the schools are more attentive to the starting salaries of their students than to the contents of the curriculum'.

The attraction of these prestigious schools is that their label is a guarantee for life, the stamp HEC-ESSEC-ESCP becomes a password for a glorious career. But the stakes are not negligible. The failure rates in reaching these schools are high - and the preparatory system leaves many people bitter or demotivated after two years of sustained effort and not even a concrete qualification to show for it - their only consolation being direct access to the second year of university courses. However, having reached the inner sanctum of the grande école, students are virtually guaranteed their diploma. As one student put it, 'In order to fail one would have to commit patricide'.(12)

Postgraduate management courses are fairly limited in number and scope. An additional year of studies is relatively popular, both with engineers trying to gain managerial insight and with management graduates seeking to specialise. The former are likely to head for an Institut d'Administration des Entreprises (IAE) course which gives a basic grounding in management. The universities also

131

cater for the other group and offer a <u>Diploma d'Etudes Supérieures Specialisées</u> (DESS) for those who already have a management background. The majority of postgraduate courses are offered by the universities.

A few of the <u>grandes écoles</u> have recently created a <u>mastères</u> which is similar to the universities' DESS in that it offers one year specialisation in a particular field. Some of the schools have also established satellite departments which offer postgraduate programs. There are only a handful of state recognised establishments and they share a common interest in exports.

Post-Experience Courses

It had been anticipated that the MBA would become as big in Europe as it was in America. In fact, its popularity was over-estimated, and INSEAD has had to diversify in order to subsidise its ailing MBA program. Originally set up specifically to provide MBA courses, INSEAD now devotes two-thirds of its faculty time to teaching managers and executives in business courses. INSEAD has had to respond to company demand for broader and more specialised programs. It has done so by offering a wide range of short courses for actual or prospective senior managers. Increasingly, INSEAD is liaising with the companies which support it, and designing tailor-made programs destined to sort out specific corporate problems.

This is a general trend in French management development programs. More and more establishments are finding they have to move closer to the work place, both intellectually and physically - not least because customised courses are highly profit-able. The tailor-made course is a booming business. Even the large consultancy organisations (CEGOS, CNOF) have been forced into providing intra-company programs since demand for standardised programs is waning. Needless to say, this fast-developing activity has engendered a new rash of small firms whose speed and versatility is well suited to tackling company-specific problems.

The schools, too, are keeping up with fashion, by being more attentive to the needs of their customers, the companies. They are developing more creative links with local companies; primarily through well-honed executive development programs and by encouraging staff to engage in consultancy

132

work. Equally important are the ties established through junior-entreprise and the increasing recourse to managers as part-time lecturers.

Most of the leading grandes écoles boast some sort of centre for management development. For the schools, this is a lucrative activity which helps to supplement income from undergraduate fees and taxe professionelle from the companies. It only represents a marginal cost since they have the facilities and staff at their disposal, not to mention a ready-made reputation. The school's renown will be exploited to attract executives to it - sometimes in search of a label they missed out on earlier in their education.

In France though, no label earned at post-entry level will really make up for inadequacies in pre-entry education. Even the most prestigious establishments for senior executives such as the CPA, INSEAD, ISA, ISSEC, CRC or CEDEP will only partly compensate a 'second rate' education. A post-entry diploma has a remedial aspect to it. It may give an engineer a managerial veneer but it will do nothing to augment the marketability of a graduate from the top grandes écoles. This is not a reflection on the pedagogy of these executive-development centres but is a sign of the deference accorded to the top schools.

[handwritten margin note: One Staff Society!]

DISTINCTIVE FEATURES OF FRENCH MANAGEMENT EDUCATION

The French management education system is a product of the society which nurtured it and shares many of its features.

To start with, the education system is elitist. It is hypersensitive and promotes a minority, giving them an employment passport through to retirement. In fact, there is growing concern voiced about the psychological effects on French society of such a system. It leaves a disillusioned and frustrated majority with the demotivating prospect of limited advancement since the upward limits on promotion are basically determined by the diploma held at the start of a career.

But the system is not only intellectually elitist, it is also socially discriminating. Based on a traditionally hierarchic society, management education in France is a distinctly class-bound affair. The pattern of socially-biased recruitment was set by the engineering schools in the eighteenth century using Latin as a social filter.

The discipline has since changed, but the mechanism lingers on even in the business schools. Certainly, the top schools are reluctant to divulge statistics on the socio-professional origins of their students. Certain sociologists(13) maintain that the educational achievements (power-merited) of the class dirigeante ('ruling class') simply serve as a smokescreen to mask its origins (power-inherited).

Management education remains heavily biased towards the higher social classes and does not appear to be making any great contributions to the democratisation of management. Nor are there any signs of change, with the grandes écoles jealously guarding their prestige by limiting the growth of successive intakes. The barely perceptible rise in output of grandes écoles graduates is in stark contrast to the continual increases in university subscriptions. The elitist tradition shows no real signs of weakening.

Nor does this status-consciousness lessen on entering a company. Executives remain acutely aware of their relative positions, based a priori on educational pedigree. It is inconceivable, for instance, that management development courses should mix people from different levels since the learning experience is a time of uncertainty, a situation where weaknesses are exposed. Strict delineation of the strata insures against loss of face before subordinates. Of course, segregation will be officially justified on more impersonal grounds, such as the need to keep groups homogeneous in terms of responsibilities. Consequently, management development courses tend to reinforce, rather than upset the managerial status quo.

Another feature of management education which is anchored in French culture is the premium placed on intellect. Intellectual merit has long been the accepted criterion for inclusion among the decision-makers of French society. France is governed by its star pupil, and the higher reaches of management are no exception. Inequalities of power can be justified by educational attainments - a less invidious credential to invoke in a democracy than either hereditary privilege or the acquisition of wealth. Thus it is, that, from the baccalauréat onwards, mathematics is the critical discipline. What more impartial criterion could one ask? Even if its relation to management does raise questions about compatibility or means and ends.

The road to success is clearly sign-posted. To keep their options open, students are best advised to pursue mathematics to the limits of their potential, irrespective of vocational preferences. It is taken for granted that anyone capable of attending X or HEC will do so, because of the tremendous career advantages it confers on them. It is achievement in the educational field which sets the elite apart. This indicates status and competence in much the same way as an individual's salary situates a person in the US.

Of late, this intellectual tradition has translated itself into 'diploma disease'. In order to ward off fears of unemployment there is a demand, which schools and universities are meeting, for lengthening curricula. But the value of protracted studies is relative and, because the tendency is widespread, companies have merely responded by raising their recruitment benchmark from baccalauréat level, to bac plus deux (years). The importance and relevance of management qualifications was neatly summed up in the epigram, 'With one you can do nothing, without one you can get nowhere'.(14)

Qualifications, and the solidarity of old boy networks, minimise the importance of a track record. Grandes écoles graduates can look forward, not only to a 'golden hello' but to rapid promotion, not always based on results. Whilst it appears unfair, this practice is accepted by all parties because the criteria used are unequivocal and known to all. Educational credentials are ideal props for hierarchical authority since they are verifiable discriminators of the organisational pecking-order. A grande école graduate is demonstrably 'better' than his organisational subordinates. Thus, elitism and the French preoccupation with egalitarianism are reconciled, since the systematic testing of individual merit gives everyone (in theory) the same opportunity of access to the elite. Intellectual superiority is deemed an acceptable ground for social differentiation.

However, in keeping with another French tradition, once a situation is acquired, it is for ever. Access to the corridors of power is on a one-shot basis. If one misses the boat as an adolescent, the chances of recovery later are remote. In effect, this is merely a variant on the French notion that benefits are cumulative and once earned, become droits acquis (acquired rights). Consistent with this, once managers attain a position, they are entrenched and can only move up.(15)

In contrast with the USA, in France the acceptance of perfectibility is low. French education is directed towards the acquisition of a well-established body of knowledge and attitudes based primarily on history and the traditional thinking of a rural society. This finite view of education has, rather inappropriately, foisted itself upon the discipline of management. By implication, anyone having attended HEC-ESSEC-ESCP, is deemed <u>formé à vie</u> (formed for life), and <u>up-dating of the great truths imparted by those schools is considered superfluous.</u> Subsequent achievements in one's job therefore count for little compared to one's schooling. In fact, the primacy of the diploma is corroborated by a cursory glance at the 'Appointments' section in newspapers. Newly appointed Chief Executive Officers will place a diploma gained several decades past ahead of their penultimate posting in a prestigious company.

This extensive (not to say exclusive) reliance on pre-experience management education, allows the brightest prospects to be creamed-off early and guarantees a safe and homogeneous product. But it also instils a superiority complex, whereby exaggerated salary and promotional expectations are founded solely on attendance at the 'right' school.

Graduates are expected to be competent when they arrive and are often appointed directly to a position of <u>cadre</u>. Ironically, this rather premature allocation of responsibilities can be just as demotivating for the lucky few as for those excluded. The former see little need to prove themselves since they are already guaranteed preferential career advancements, whilst the latter must resign themselves to an atrophied career.

The French also show a great fondness for hierarchies. The obsession with classification is visible in the star system for ranking cooks and couturiers, in the penchant for civilian medals and in the importance of finalists ranking (<u>classement</u>) in the top <u>grandes écoles</u>. The higher the league position, the higher the signing-on fee commanded by its graduates. Whilst salaries are often exorbitant, companies tend to play along, safe in the knowledge that they are acquiring the brightest possible personnel. <u>Companies are apt to look upon the grandes écoles as elaborate sifting systems rather than purveyors of knowledge - and many make no secret of the fact that they are effectively purchasing the concours</u> (entrance exam).

In this respect, companies merely endorse the view of qualifications as 'entry tickets'. Of course, access to business is not associated with qualification embodying a job-specific content, in the same way as access to architecture, medicine or law. But French companies seem to push this argument to excess. Most employers would still favour products of X (engineers) or l'ENA (civil servants) to their HEC counterparts (managers). Strictly speaking, the first two were not designed to train managers for private enterprise but both students and employers treat them as such. Students intent on a career in industry will have no qualms about heading for these schools, whose label is an open-sesame to all careers. Moreover, their legitimacy is enhanced by the philosophical viewpoint that the practice of management (as opposed to its theoretical concepts) cannot be taught.

To develop this last idea, there is a deep rooted belief in France that managers are born not made. As Dominique Xardel, the Directeur of l'ESSEC (part of the top trio of management schools), put it: 'Let's be clear; in a school one acquires information, one can develop aptitudes already existing in an embryonic state, but one can hardly create them'.(16) Training can only bring out innate talent, it cannot generate it spontaneously. A grande école education of any sort is regarded as a useful apprenticeship to management - what the products lack in technique they make up for in psychological preparation for leadership. In spite of a slight erosion of the gap between engineering and commercial schools, the former remain dominant on employers' 'hit lists' and have shown their intentions of retaining pole position by including business options in their curricula.

In many cases, added value may be obtained from entering public service(17) and using one's privileged knowledge of its workings as a springboard for a second career in industry and the donning of 'golden slippers' (pantouflage). It is a sign of their relatively smooth transition that the extent of the phenomenon is so little known, primarily because the social background and training of senior civil servants bring them close to the business elite. The passage amounts to professional mobility, but within the same social field, hence its success.

The headline-grabbing instances of pantouflage, associated with nationalised companies and changes of government are simply the tip of the iceberg.

Beneath the surface there is a steady, osmotic flow from the public sector (including the armed forces) to the private sector. The pattern is a classic one. Transfer usually takes place in the mid-thirties, by which time the cadre has ample public sector experience to offer as well as an appreciation of career limitations (in public service), yet sufficient drive left to make an impact in the private sector.

The circumstances for leaving vary. Some respond to an offer, others take the initiative, having carefully cultivated contacts when in office. Either way, ex-civil servants have numerous trumps to play with prospective employers. They possess intimate knowledge of the rules and regulations. They have friends in high places and can facilitate dialogue with those who administer. What is more, even if they cannot play on personal contacts or are dealing with an unfamiliar field, they know how to lobby and, having themselves been on the receiving end, know when and where to apply pressure. Nor should one neglect their high-level training which permits a rapid grasp of complex problems. In the French context at least, ex-civil servants clearly have something to offer most employers.

The most sought after specialists are the inspecteurs des finances (glorified accountants) who virtually monopolise the higher reaches of the banking sector. Demand for members of the other key administrative functions (les grands corps) also exceeds supply since these are positions acquired with difficulty and left reluctantly. In terms of numbers, the foremost pantoufleurs are ex-service personnel, who can foresee their likely baton de maréchal (promotional ceiling) and find a natural outlet in the armaments or electronics sectors. A few large companies can even boast their own clan of St Cyriens (18) to go alongside groups from X, Centrale or Arts et Métiers. Occasionally, civil servants will equip themselves with a legitimising qualification prior to making the transition. A diploma from the Centre de Perfectionnement aux Affaires (CPA) is a particular favourite, since it bestows prestige and a useful old boy network which spans public and private sectors.

French renown for state intervention is another trait which has manifested itself in management education. State influence in the field was fairly limited until, in typical French style, it was decided that training warranted formal national commitment. A levy was imposed on companies whereby expenditure on training had to be equivalent to 1.1 per cent of the wage bill although companies were left with entire discretion as to how, and on whom, the money should be spent (cadres are typically allocated 30 per cent of the budget). Of course, setting compulsory spending-levels underlined state enthusiasm for training, as well as providing it with annual statements of progress and a database to fuel the long-term thinking of government, corporations and educational institutions. However, creating a legal requirement to spend was hardly a declaration of faith vis-à-vis the companies, since it implied that they would not undertake training on a voluntary basis.

In keeping with the general pattern of French social and economic and political life, the provision for management education is heavily concentrated in and around Paris. In provincial France, with the exception of Lyon, the second city, higher management education is relatively weak - not least because the two-tier higher education system (universities/grandes écoles) dilutes the available intellectual and financial resources. A recent survey by l'Expansion(19) condemned French business school libraries as unworthy of the name. Only HEC and l'ESSEC met with its approval in this domain. Moreover, students hoping to be admitted to the trio of top commercial schools (les grandes parisiennes), head for the Parisian preparatory schools described earlier, which afford the best chances of success. Parisian domination is made complete by the fact that the CCIP is the most influential sponsor of French management education. Obviously, the geographical concentration does not favour the democratisation of French management.

Another recurrent feature of French business and politics is the institutionalisation of communication. The archetypal example is, of course, the National Plan, though a more commonplace manifestation is the French predilection for formal business meetings, sometimes condemned as la réunionite ('meeting-itis'). The goal sought in either case is to set up a framework which ensures a dialogue between parties who might not communicate if left to their own devices. The field of management education offers two such examples: the FNEGE and the Chambers of Commerce and Industry (CCIs).

The FNEGE unites several parties (CCIs, CNPF, state) in its council thereby providing a platform for dialogue and exchange between course directors, senior managers and senior civil servants. At its inception, the foundation basically administered grants destined to assist in the training of staff and the professionalisation of management education. But, progressively, it has become more active in the setting up of new schools and in encouraging co-operation between schools. The foundation remains an influential co-ordinator but it now provides practical, as well as financial, support; its outlook has shifted from arm's length to hands on.

Whilst the FNEGE has championed the need for management education in France, it has been the Chambers of Commerce and Industry (CCIs) which have been the foremost activists in the field. Although financed by taxes, they are independent in their actions and lend coherence to the system by their presence at all levels. For instance, they are heavily involved in the provision of practical, low cost courses at regional levels aimed at small, owner-managed units. They also provide vocational one-year courses for students having completed their baccalauréat. At the other end of the spectrum, most of the notable commercial grandes écoles fall under the auspices of the CCIs which gives them a say in the management development programs offered by the business schools. Most notable among the CCIs is, of course, the CCIP which has hatched France's most coveted management schools as well as helping to launch the foremost executive-education centers like the CPA, ISA and INSEAD. The relationship between schools and industry is, therefore, guaranteed via the CCIs, which are run by representatives of business who are indirectly engaged in the administration of the schools.

OVERVIEW AND FUTURE

France bought its business education on the cheap. It drew extensively from proven methods developed in the US. Spared the trial and error process, France was able to make significant progress in a short space of time. The three decades which followed World War II, labelled les trente glorieuses(20), constituted a radical improvement in French competitiveness and, in the process, helped management education to gain its lettres de noblesse. However, the close association between this economic boom and the influx of American management concepts encouraged indiscriminate transplantation, without serious consideration of applicability to French culture. In fact, it was probably infatuation for American methods and ideas which precipitated their demise.

The first reservations were expressed in the early 1970s and manifested themselves in a curbing of French enthusiasm for American MBAs. From 1974 onwards, the FNEGE, in particular, started to train prospective management teachers in France or Europe rather than in the US. There was a realisation that France had to move towards a more European focus and develop materials, pedagogies and institutions suited to national needs rather than naively attempting to recreate French Harvards, The point was driven home by translated case studies borrowed from the US with its less complex social structure and a more liberal economic system; tackling issues such as hiring and firing à l'américaine, was unthinkable in the French context.

French management education was now firmly established as a respectable discipline and, armed with its newly-formed body of management teachers, could afford to kick away the American crutch. Effectively, France was realising the limitations of a universalist approach and was shifting to a particularist stance - from the assumption that a single model of management practice and education could be applied to the belief that these should be shaped by national needs. A few schools such as l'Ecole Européene des Affaires (EAP) gave the lead by building up worthwhile exchanges with European universities instead of fashionable links with American ones.

The fact remains however, that French management education has still not really shaken off its American colouration. Its difficulty in imposing its own identity owes much to the impoverished nature of management research(21). This is in part a legacy of the two-tier system in which the foremost training establishments, the grandes écoles, are too small to carry out meaningful research - the most innovative work being performed in universities. Management research also suffers from traditional scepticism concerning the relevance of the output to practising managers.

Part of the problem is, therefore, a product of the circumstances. More worrying,however, is the realisation that the low status of researchers is to some extent self-inflicted. Sclerosis has set into the profession of management education, largely as a result of France's excessive haste in appropriating for itself a corps of qualified management teachers. Because they were sent off in droves throughout the early 70s, there is now a glut of middle-aged management teachers with guaranteed employment through to retirement. They are disillusioned by lack of recognition for their profession and unstimulated by the dearth of young pretenders. The problem is exacerbated by a stifling career-structure which mitigates against those who wish to spend practical periods out in industry.

There is hope, however, in the intensity of the movement towards 'in-house' education by French business schools, which outstrip their US counterparts in this domain. Company demand in France is so strong that several of the leading business schools could occupy their full teaching capacity exclusively with in-company programs. Inevitably, this increased collaboration is perpetuating spin-off research projects. Two-way relationships between faculty and firm can only contribute to the increasing relevance and appreciation of management research, which augers well for the future of management education as a profession.

National commitment to adult education, inaugurated in 1971, is starting to bear fruit. Initially, companies were prone to treat this as an unwelcome chore because of the difficulties associated with application, not least the compilation of statistics for the government. Small firms, in particular, are unable to detach someone full-time to deal with the administration, so the Chief Executive Officer (general 'dogsbody' in small companies) is wont to take the task upon himself.

Deciding who should attend which course and when is quite onerous, as well as politically explosive, and must be reconciled with conflicting pressures on the CEO's time. Trying to please everyone is not easy and, without full information about available courses, the training budget tends to become a slush-fund used to indulge meritorious or restless cadres by sending them off on courses. A provincial cadre will look upon a few days in Paris as a 'perk' and notification that he is on the fast track. Alternatively, the training budget may be used as a panacea for a longstanding problem - an individual may be sent off on what is termed un stage alibi, whereby subsequent crises will not be attributable to inadequate training. So training becomes a piecemeal affair destined to facilitate IR and keep individuals as well as the works committee happy.

The problem is compounded for smaller companies by the fact that they can ill afford to be deprived of their top cadres for lengthy spells. What is more, training represents a danger for the company since it puts its prime talent on display and at the mercy of potential poachers. Why release a cadre into a tempting environment where he will sound-out opportunities and, more importantly, gain a qualification negotiable on the open market? Worse still, those sent on courses might return in positions to challenge existing practices and either cause upheaval or feel frustrated at not being given free reign to apply what they have learnt. For sound practical reasons, therefore, many small companies have dispensed with the burden in the most expeditious way, by paying the balance to a recognised training body or, as a last resort, to the Treasury.

Increasingly even small companies are beginning to come to grips with the training levy. Gone is the era of general courses for self-development or interest which conveniently satisfied the legal obligation. Companies are starting to realise that practical gain can be derived from incorporating training into their long-term strategies. This is corroborated by the appointment of training personnel, to prepare statements of intent (submitted for works council approval) and make more efficient use of the budget through better information of training opportunities. A professional association (GARF)(22) has even been created to lend weight to the profession. Nonetheless, the title responsable (as opposed to directeur) betrays the fact that this remains a low prestige function - one to be avoided by budding directors.

Although the salary gap between commercial and engineering graduates is constantly being eroded, companies continue to show a preference for the latter - engineering methods are still entrusted with the making of French managers, even if they no longer hold a monopoly. Companies are still willing to pay back a polytechnicien's fees to the state in order to capture him immediately on graduation and spare him ten years purgatory in state service.

Whilst pantouflage shows no signs of flagging, an interesting twist has been added to the practice by the Industry Minister, Edouard Balladur. To underline his commitment to free market policies, he has broken with tradition and appointed Jacques Maisonrouge, the former Chairman of IBM Europe, to a key post in the French administration. The choice was a symbolic tribute on the part of the government to US business and has, at least, put an end to the one-way traffic from public to private sector. However, it seems unlikely that the trend will warrant a new appellation.

There are other developments in the offing, notably a convergence between business and engineering schools. Under the impetus of the FNEGE, new commercial schools have been established at Grenoble and Belfort which have a high technological input. In a similar vein, HEC has developed a high-technology program for five or six students per year to go away to the foremost American universities to study scientific subjects. There are also signs of collaboration between rival business and engineering schools; the tightening relationship between the Ecole Supérieur de Commerce and the Ecole Centrale, both situated in Lyon, is a conspicuous example.

CONCLUSION

Any attempt to identify the merits and shortcomings of French management education is fraught with difficulty since each distinguishing feature seems to embody both. The grandes écoles, for instance, are at once credited with elevating France to its present economic prosperity and blamed for the failings of the economic machine. To a greater extent than most nations, the French system of management education seems to have the weakness of its strengths (and vice versa):

> The highly-selective educational system earmarks high flyers for early responsibility and rapid promotion. This facilitates their learning process but leaves those excluded with the prospect of limited advancement. The grandes écoles have contributed to the academisation of management at the expense of a broader recruiting base.

> The policy of using the grandes écoles to form pools of versatile talent avoids type-casting, promotes mobility and facilitates dialogue between educational, business, financial, and public sectors; but means that these leaders for every occasion need much longer to be

operationally effective and, indeed, may never be so, skating over the surface until they are sucked-up to the boardroom. The pre-eminence of pre-experience education condemns post-experience education to a subordinate place since perfectibility is deemed minimal. The existing provision for management education seems an accurate reflection of this dominance (hence the relative space devoted to them above). Like a zero-sum game, one part of the system is strong at the expense of the other.

Mathematics, as a culturally-neutral and precisely-quantifiable criterion, is employed as an objective measure of merit for entry into the commercial schools; but in the process the elements of scholastic success are uncoupled from those of professional success. In effect, the entry-filter is placed at the stage where teaching is at its most theoretical, thereby excluding pragmatic or artistically-inclined individuals.

The route to the top is clearly signposted which minimises the risks of losing potential talent through misinformation - but the price paid is a sheeplike procession towards the same schools and a snubbing of vocational courses. Worse still, competition to enter is so keen and the subsequent gains so automatic, that admission to the grandes écoles is perceived as a landing rather than a take-off point.

High-flyer schemes, to which the elite are privy, help to develop standardised management talent but encourage young executives to look good and avoid trouble rather than exploit their capacities.

Obligatory spending on training has, perhaps, delayed the establishment of a management development ethos, with small firms more concerned about minimising the concomitant problems than trying to spend the money wisely.

Concentration of the most prestigious establishments in Paris is intellectually stimulating but is not conducive to the dissemination of good management practice.

Management education is a great force for change but it is also a prisoner of the society in which it evolves. France remains a strongly hierarchic society and management education operates within that framework. The French model has made significant progress since World War II but it is still a long way from democratic perfection. Many of the social filters associated with the embryonic grandes écoles system still exist, albeit under different guises. For the time being, then, the verdict must be, plus ça change.

GLOSSARY OF ABBREVIATIONS IN FRENCH MANAGEMENT EDUCATION

Bac	Baccalauréat - equivalent of 'A' levels
CCI	Chambre(s) de Commerce et d'Industrie
CCIP	Chambre de Commerce et d'Industrie de Paris
CEDEP	Centre Européen d'Education Permanente
CEGOS	Commission Générale d'Organisation Scientifique
Centrale	L'Ecole Centrale - private engineering <u>grande école</u>
CNOF	Comité Nationale de l'Organisation Francaise
CNPF	Conseil National du Patronat Francais
CPA	Centre de Perfectionnement aux Affaires
CRC	Centre de Recherches et d'Etudes des Chefs d'Entreprises
Dauphine	Management University, Paris-IX,
DESS	Diplôme d'Etudes Supérieures Specialisées
EAP	Ecole des Affaires de Paris/Ecole Européene des Affaires
ENA	Ecole Nationale d'Administration
ENE	Ecole Nationale d'Exportation
ESCAE	Ecole(s) Supérieure(s) de Commerce et d'Administration des Entreprises
ESSEC	Ecole Supérieure des Sciences Economiques et Commerciales
FNEGE	Fondation Nationale pour l'Enseignement de la Gestion des Entreprises
GARF	Groupement des Agents Responsables de la Formation

Management Education in France

HEC	Ecole des Hautes Etudes Commerciales
IAE	Institut(s) d'Administration des Entreprises
IFG	Institut Français de Gestion
INSEAD	Institut Européen d'Administration des Affaires
ISA	Institut Supérieur des Affaires
ISSEC	Institut Supérieur de Sciences Economiques et Commerciales (groupe ESSEC)
IUT	Institut(s) Universitaire(s) de Technologie
X	L'Ecole Polytechnique

NOTES

1. Graduate of the archetypal _grande école, l'Ecole Politechnique,_ known as X because of its emblem bearing two crossed cannons.
2. French management education is littered with acronyms. A glossary of abbreviations lists these at the end of the chapter.
3. Ecoles Supérieures de Commerce et d'Administration des Entreprises, more prosaically known as Sup-de-Co.
4. Commission Générale d'Organisation Scientifique.
5. Story & Parrott, _International Herald Tribune_, 5 May 1977, 'An Essay on Management in France - Does it Work?'
6. HEC had briefly experimented with case studies in 1928 but had found them unsuited to the spirit of the school.
7. The status of _cadre_ was adopted from the military context and transferred to the business setting in the 1930s.
8. Ecole Nationale d'Administration - Elite public administration school set up in 1945 to supply senior civil servants.
9. University programs at Aix-en-Provence, Bordeaux, Grenoble, Lille, Lyon and Renne. Grandes écoles programs at HEC and ESSEC.
10. A three year vocational course, not to be confused with the one year specialist course, the mastères offered by selected grandes écoles.
11. Established in 1925, taxe professionnelle is a levy on companies which they may donate to any pre-entry training establishment. Its level is set at 0.6 per cent of the wage bill. Prospection and collection is left to the initiative of the students themselves.
12. 'Faut-il couler les grandes écoles?' L'Expansion, 29 October 1982, p. 121.
13. Notably P. Birnbaum: La Classe Dirigeante Française and P. Bourdieu: Les Héritiers. They contend that, by requiring managers to be super-numerate, access is biased towards well-off students who benefit from earlier apprenticeship to abstraction.
14. Jacques Fontaine: 'Les grandes entreprises jugent les grandes écoles', L'Expansion July/August 1977.
15. Francois de Closets' best-seller, Toujours Plus is full of examples.

16.   Quoted in Whitley, Thomas & Marceau: p. 67 <u>Master of Business</u>.

17.   A civil service career is still prestigous but, increasingly, it is regarded as a short-cut to senior positions in the private or nationalised sectors, rather than an end in itself.

18.   St Cyr - French equivalent of West Point or Sandhurst.

19.   'Le Hit-Parade des Ecoles de Commerce', <u>L'Expansion</u> 6/19 March 1987.

20.   J. Fourastié, <u>Les Trente Glorieuses,</u> Fayard, 1979.

21.   'La Revue Française de Gestion', published by the FNEGE stands out as France's sole well-known refereed management journal.

22.   Groupement des Agents Responsables de Formation.

Chapter Seven

MANAGEMENT EDUCATION IN WEST GERMANY
Peter Lawrence

Management education in Germany is determined by
the German concept of management, and this is
significantly different to that prevailing in the
English-speaking world.
    The crucial ways in which the German under-
standing of management differs are:

- Germans have a relatively weak concept of
  management.
- Their emphasis is on the specialist rather than
  generalist.
- German management is strongly technical.

It will help to set the scene to enlarge on these
global characteristic differences.

A WEAK CONCEPT OF MANAGEMENT

There is less writing, thinking, and talking about
management _per se_ in West Germany, compared with
other advanced industrial countries. The ideal of
the professional manager developed late in Germany
and it is significant that a foreign rather than
indigenous word is used. In the early days
'manager' was a term used for those who 'stage
managed' circuses or prize fights, rather than for
captains of industry. In the German scheme of
things, managers suffered by comparison with entrepreneurs (Untermehmer) and it is interesting that,
although the Germans do not have an indigenous word
for manager, they have their own word, Untermehmer

151

for entrepreneurs and do not use an imported French word, as do the Americans and the British.

The <u>Untermehmer</u>, rather than the manager, is the traditional focus of respect in German society. The <u>Untermehmer</u> is respected not only for using his capital in a business venture but also for his presumptive personal control and responsibility. All this is still reflected in the use of language: it would be possible to say <u>managerhaft</u> (managerial) in German but people do not say it, instead the word <u>untermehmerisch</u> (entrepreneurial) is used and with distinct laudatory overtones. A manager whose conduct is described as <u>untermehmerisch</u> is an undoubted 'good guy' who has acted with the interests of the company at heart.

But can one pull these considerations into the late twentieth century and ask: 'So what; does it make any difference now?' The answer is 'yes'. Germans have a much weaker conviction that there is something separate, definable, and objective called management. They doubt that one can really extrapolate this aspect of a variety of tasks and label it separately, dissect it, make generalisations about it, offer exhortations concerning it - and provide a disembodied, generalised training in it. In Germany you do not manage, you manage something.

This orientation has numerous results. There is no indigenous classical management literature in Germany, of the French, British, or American kind (nor is there any indigenous 'how to get to the top in business without really trying' literature - although some of the Anglo-Saxon classics are read in translation). German management thinking and practice is relatively immune to American influence and the power of American example is less lauded than in, say, Britain in the 1950s or France in the 1960s.

There are, strictly speaking, no undergraduate courses in management or business administration; the nearest approach, business economics, will be discussed later. There are no MBAs and, indeed, no masters degrees at all, in the sense of a qualification, between the bachelor and doctor degree level (the unwary are sometimes tricked by the fact that at some German universities the bachelors degree is called a Masters - in Latin!). Nor are we concerned here just with differences in the use of terms and labels; West Germany offers no immediate postgraduate courses in management of any kind.

To complete the picture, Germany also lacks business schools. Business schools are not an exclusively Anglo-Saxon phenomenon, witness, for example, IMEDE in Switzerland, INSEAD in France, or even Nijenrode in the Netherlands(1). Furthermore, the under-representation of German managers at business schools abroad has been noted in the 1970's(2) and again in the 1980's(3).

SPECIALIST RATHER THAN GENERALIST

The Anglo-Saxon approach to management is a broadly generalist one(4). We believe that management ability is general and transferable; we believe in management science, principles of management and the legitimacy of generalisations about management. At the level of the individual, American managers believe they can 'manage anything' while British managers are pleased to be called 'good all-rounders'. Management mobility - between functions, companies, even branches of industry - is held to be 'a good thing', indeed at least a modicum of inter-company mobility is taken as a trademark of ambition and an indicator of eventual success. What is more, this career mobility is accompanied by geographic mobility and companies often make a point of moving people - a career progression mixed with rite de passage. In the United States and Great Britain there are no formal barriers to such geographic mobility, only considerations of family, preferences and convenience. There is much less of all this in West Germany.

German managers tend to think of specific jobs (and specific training for them). Their attitudes to mobility are coloured by specific considerations: a move from a quality control job in a fork-lift truck plant to a quality control job in a rival fork lift truck company is conceivable (although you have to have a reason for doing it), but flitting from chemicals to mechanical engineering is not conceivable, even in a traditionally mobile function such as sales(5).

Germans tend to use specific job titles/ descriptions and eschew general ones (like manager!). A German tells you:

'Ich bin Konstrukteur' (I am a designer)
'Ich bin Verkaufsleiter' (I am a sales manager)
'Ich bin in der Vorschung und Entwicklung tätig' (I work in R & D).

Similarly, they tend to give product or more activity-related accounts of their jobs:

'We make and sell fork lift trucks'
rather than:
'I coordinate the functional contributions and devise policy'.

Germans take management jobs seriously but, at the same time, they have a rather straight-forward view of them. You take a relevant qualification in terms of its content, start in a job area for which your study has prepared you, and stick with it. Careers develop within functions - personnel, sales production, and so on, typically in a particular industry and sometimes in a single company. General management is less general and it starts at a higher level. This has a clear organisational manifestation.

In his comparative study of the nature of the control function in companies in Britain, France and Germany, Horovitz notes the prevalence of the functional organisational form in Germany. German companies are kept big, with one big sales department and one big design department, and so on, with a super-functional co-ordination only at the point of the pyramid(6). Sorge has underlined the same phenomenon, noting the relative absence of divisionalisation, American-style, among German companies. Nor are Germans concerned to break up companies into 'manageable units', in contrast to Britain where, as Sorge puts it, 'enterprise management became the specialism of the generalists'(7).

The result of their specialist orientation is that management training assumes a specific form. Much of it is done by companies themselves rather than delegated to the state education system, and the company-offering, of which more later, tends to be specific as to content and audience.

TECHNIK ÜBER ALLES

There is a persistent dominance of engineers and technical considerations in German industry(8). Indeed in the country that is famous for its virtuosity at, and interest in, making things, this technical orientation is manifest even in ways that Germans think about bodies of knowledge, subjects and the relation between them.

The conventional distinction between the arts

and sciences, immortalised by the late Sir Charles Snow(9), poses a problem for engineering in that it does not fit neatly under either heading. The Anglo-Saxon solution has been to label engineering as 'applied science', a nom de convenance, which is actually questionable on several grounds:

- it fails to distinguish between the output of science which is codified knowledge and the output of engineering which is three-dimensional artifacts
- it posits a dependent relationship for engineering, whereas advances in engineering are not invariably dependent on prior advances in science
- it is not only obfuscating, but mildly demeaning for engineering.

The rival German schema simply by-passes this mine-field of misapprehension. German thinking distinguishes between:

- Wissenschaft, which denotes formal-knowledge subjects, whether arts, science or social science in our terms.
- Kunst, which is art, but the output and practice of the arts, not 'the arts subjects' as in the English-speaking world.
- Technik, the knowledge and skill relating to manufacturing, that is to say, engineering knowledge and craft skills.

Thus, the German Technik formulation not only avoids the demeaning connotations of applied science but positively valorises engineering under an independent rubric.(10)

If this discussion of the way in which Germans perceive bodies of knowledge is held to be 'all in the mind' it must be said that the pre-eminence of engineering in Germany has some very tangible manifestations as well. More German managers are qualified in engineering than in anything else; engineers are well represented on the boards of companies and among the ranks of chief executives, if only by sheer weight of numbers. There is even a study(11) which shows that:

- Managers on the technical side are better qualified than managers on the commercial side

-   qualified engineers dominate the technical functions - production, design, R & D, engineering, quality control, etc.
-   they also overspill into the non-technical functions - sales, marketing, costing, purchasing, personnel, central planning, but the reverse is not true.

If we take together the last two arguments, the dominance of the specialist over the generalist and of the technical over the commercial, then much recruitment of actual or potential managers into German companies proceeds in terms of the specifics of prior education. Thus, for example, the chemical industry does not recruit graduates in general, where ability to reach degree-standard is seen as promising a general level of intellectual ability and learning capacity; chemical companies recruit graduates in chemistry and chemical engineering (and they typically have a doctorate as well). Or more generally, graduates (especially engineers) are recruited not just for their degree grades but for the specific content of their courses, with personnel officers being surprisingly knowledgeable about university syllabuses. Indeed recruitment interviews may well focus on what elective subjects the applicant chose at university and their presumptive relevance to the company's operations, or what the student wrote his Diplomarbeit (undergraduate dissertation, final year) on and its potential relevance.

FROM MANAGEMENT TO TRAINING

The three considerations which have been argued in the brief sketch of German management above - weak concept of management, specialism and technical orientation - are less discrete than we have depicted them, they overlap and interpenetrate. Taken together, they have several implications for a study of management education in Germany. First, they mean that in Germany people are educated for management rather than trained in management. Second, to understand what training de facto managers have had, one needs to look at a wider spectrum of educational provision. Third, much of this educational provision will be in the form of specific vocational preparation rather than explicit management education.

ENGINEERING AND MANAGEMENT

Given the de facto dominance of engineers referred to in the previous section, it is worth considering, albeit briefly, the nature of engineering education in West Germany, with particular attention to its relative strengths.

Most university-level engineering education occurs in the separate Technische Hochschulen or technical universities. Students typically enter these at 19 years of age, having passed the Abitur exam, which is broader based, and with less (premature) subject-dropping than with, for example, 'A' level GCE in Britain. It is also the case that the Abitur grades of Germans who go on to study engineering at university compare well with those who elect to study other subjects(12) whereas, in Britain, the relative inferiority of engineering students in this respect has been documented in the past(13).

German universities require engineering students to complete a six-month practical placement in industry, and this is a universal and mandatory requirement (it is not in Britain). German engineering courses at university level are further differentiated from those in Britain by being:

-   longer; the official length of the course is four years, but actual, average completion-time is 5.8 years
-   by spending less syllabus time on basic engineering science
-   by spending less time on non-technical subjects
-   by spending more time on design
-   by spending more time on various specialisms
-   by the mandatory requirement to produce a Diplomarbeit or final year dissertation; its subject may be either theoretical or practical although the typical Diplomarbeit is probably on a practical issue of interest to industry (with the practical work being done at a company rather than in the university's laboratory).

Another strength of German university-level engineering education is the integration between industry and the Technische Hochschulen. Apart from the links occasioned by the mandatory practical training and often by the Diplomarbeit described above, there is a connection in terms of leading personnel. The typical career path for a

German engineering professor goes something like this. First degree (Dipl.Ing.) in engineering followed by a doctor's degree (Dr.Ing.). Then leave the university and into industry, not for a year or two, but more likely for something between six to twelve years, often moving from a research or design activity to a technical administration or general management role. Then, back into the university system at the level of full professor.

Below the university level in Germany are a range of subject qualifications obtained at colleges known as Fachhochschulen. Entry to a Fachhochschule engineering course is normally at the age of 18. The route is normally one of leaving a non-selective or semi-selective secondary school at 16 with the mittlere Reife examination (roughly equivalent to G.C.E. 'O' level in England), and spending two years at an intermediate technical college (Fachoberschule), obtaining the entry qualifications for the Fachhochschule (the Fachoberschule course also includes a short practical). The engineering course at the Fachhochschule is for three years, full-time, including another short practical, and a compulsory thesis along the lines of the Diplomarbeit at university level. The resulting qualification at the end of the course is that of graduierter Ingenieur or, in the conventional abbreviated form, Ing.(grad.).

The raison d'etre for the Fachhochschule course is that it is reckoned to be more practical, more directly oriented to industry's operational needs. (There used to be a quip in German that the economic miracle of the 1950s and 1960s was the achievement of the Ing.(grad.) assisted by the ex-Wehrmacht infantry officer as industrial salesmen. The Ing.(grad.) tends to fill positions in industry in design and production, with the Dipl.Ing. going into R & D and (eventually) general management.

The Fachhochschulen are also well integrated with industry, not only by their avowed and evident practicality, but also by their lecturing staff. The Fachhochschule lecturer is required by law to be a university graduate (Dipl.Ing. in the case of engineering lecturers) and to have a minimum of five years experience in industry. This simple law is a masterly act of practical integration.

Summing up, the strengths of engineering education in Germany include:

158

- good preparation for engineering study, high
  standards, avoidance of over-specialisation at
  school
- substantial courses, longer than their equiva-
  lents in, say, Britain or the USA
- strong in practice
- strong in design
- good relations between the engineering
  education establishment and industry.

LAW AND MANAGEMENT POSTS

Surveys of the qualifications of German management
indicate that, among the university graduates,
engineers are the largest single group, with the
remainder being more or less equally divided
between lawyers and economists, with only very
small numbers of graduates in anything else (outside the chemical industry). Law graduates are
fairly common among the ranks of German management,
but not distributed at random. They are, in proportion to their numbers, frequently found at or
near the top; they are common on the Aufsichtsrat
(supervisory board) as opposed to the Vorstand
(executive committee). They are also well
represented in banking and insurance, as opposed to
manufacturing industry.

The German deployment of qualified lawyers in
management is an interesting exception to our
earlier comments on the German preference for the
specialist (and the technical). Lawyers are to be
valued precisely in terms of their general attributes: - reasoning ability, trained intelligence,
ability to 'make a case' and objectivity, facilitating judgment and overview. With regard to the
consistency of German preferences, however, there
are some qualifications to be made. First, an
exception to the generalist interpretation is to be
found in the case of lawyers in personnel administration. The traditional qualification for the
personnel manager is a first degree and doctorate
in law. But personnel work in German companies is
much more legalistic than in the USA or Britain;
the German personnel manager is to a much higher
degree engaged in applying the law in the company -
law on conditions, safety, worker representation,
and so on.(14)

Second, for the reader who is thinking that, if
the Germans are prepared to depart from their
specialist principles in favour of lawyers, why no

history, classics and philosophy graduates too (as in story-book England)? There is a counter-argument to be made, in favour of continental rather than just German law studies. That is, in England, former British colonies, and the English speaking world generally, the predominance of case or precedent law puts a burden on memory, rote-learning, and fact-detail acquisition. On the continent, however, the predominance of codified law eliminates the rote-learning burden (you can go away and look it up!) and means that law studies are stronger on philosophy, ethics, sociology, logic and so on; are more mind-expanding. So that if one is, albeit exceptionally, going down the generalist road, continental law studies are a good preparation.

The third qualification is to say that, although the incorporation of law graduates into (general) management may not be instantly familiar in the English-speaking world, the phenomenon we have outlined for Germany is by no means unique to that country. The same would hold, at least, for Austria, Switzerland, the Netherlands, and Scandinavia; for example the head of Volvo, Pehr Gyllenhammar, is a lawyer.

ECONOMICS & MANAGEMENT

People with an economics qualification do not have a monopoly on the commercial functions in German companies(15) but they are decently represented in these areas of management work.

It should be said, straightaway, that there are two broad species of economist in the German scheme of things. There is the Volkswirt, or political economist, and the Betriebswirt (or Kaufmann), or business economist. The traditional set-up is that brighter people (better Arbitur grades etc.) enrolled for the Volkswirt courses - this was well recognised by employers who hired Volkswirte rather than Betriebswirte, in spite of the greater relevance to industry of the studies of the latter.

But by the late 1980s this has all changed. Betriebswirtschaftslehre (business economics) has become the dominant subject, and enrolments for it exceed those for Volkswirtschaft by some ten to one; also the subject's greater relevance has been recognised.

The route to a university study of Betriebswirtschaftslehre (business economics) is the same as for engineering described in an earlier section.

Study, typically at a <u>Gymnasium</u> (selective secondary school), leads to the <u>Arbitur</u> which, in turn, admits to the university. A <u>Praktikum</u>, or practical training period in commerce or industry, is required as for engineering. There is, again, a <u>Diplomarbeit,</u> or final year dissertation, and teaching staff typically have both past experience and present consultancy contact with industry and commerce.

The question naturally arises, is <u>Betriebswirtschaftslehre</u> the same as what would be called management studies or business administration in the English Speaking world? It should be said that it is not a question that permits a precise or 'black and white' answer.

Certainly there is a 'family resemblance' and substantial overlap, but it is probably fair to say that there are two levels of difference. The first is about 'where they are coming from'. Undergraduate management courses in English-speaking countries owe their existence to the conviction that management is a valid (composite) subject and that it is worth teaching. <u>Betriebswirtschaft</u> courses in Germany derive from the conviction that knowledge of economics/finance/book-keeping is necessary for running businesses(16). In short, the general is still counterposed to the particular.

The other difference is that, from conversations with German <u>Betriebswirtschaftlehre</u> teachers and on reading some syllabuses, there appears to be a patterned, partial-syllabic distinction. The German courses have more economics,book-keeping and techniques; the Anglo-Saxon courses more general management, principles of management, organisational behaviour, industrial sociology, and so on.

As with engineering, business economics is also taught at the lower <u>Fachhochschule</u> level, on the model:

<u>Mittlere Reife</u>	<u>Fachober-schule</u>	<u>Fachhoch-schule</u>	<u>Betr. (grad.)</u>
Age 16	Age 16 - 18	Age 18 - 21	Age 21
(GCE 'O' level)	(Inter-mediate technical college)	3 yrs. Full-time	(final qualification like Ing. (grad.) for engineering).

Again, as with the Fachhochschule engineering course, there is a short mandatory Praktikum (practical training period in commerce or industry), a final year project-dissertation along the lines of the Diplomarbeit at university level, and the lecturers are also all university graduates with a legally-required minimum of five years experience in commerce and industry.

APPRENTICESHIP

While apprenticeship may seem a humble topic in a discussion of management training, apprenticeship is or has been a building block in the process of qualification-acquisition for many German managers, and for some older managers it was the terminal qualification. But, before detailing the role of apprenticeship as a building block, it will probably be helpful to set the scene with an overview conjoined with a contrast with Britain, to put it into perspective.

In both Britain and Germany, apprenticeship originated in the middle ages as part of the craft-guild system. But from these comparable beginnings, the institution of apprenticeship has had a different 'career' in the two societies.

The British view related apprenticeship particularly to craft occupations and found the institution less appropriate to industrialisation(17). Apprenticeship has not had strong state-support, has been little diluted and not diversified to take account of the new occupational operations coming in with various phases of industrialisation. Indeed, the industry view is that apprenticeship is a little restrictive, a weapon for (some) employees in their struggle with management to control the terms and conditions of their employment.

The development of apprenticeships in Germany has been different. It was not seen as restrictive or inappropriate to industrialisation as opposed to craft economy. It has had government and industry backing, and apprenticeship today is controlled by the various Industrie-und Handelskammer, representing employees, employers, and educators. Furthermore, the range of occupations for which there is an apprenticeship has been enlarged over time to take account of the new occupational specialisms. The set-up, today, is that there are getting on for 500 jobs for which there is a recognised apprenticeship, right across the occupational structure - industry, banking, commerce, public sector and service.

A few more pointed contrasts with apprenticeship in Britain may again be helpful in characterising the institution in Germany. First, a German apprenticeship **always** ends with both a theoretical written examination and a practical skill- based test; this does not hold for Britain(18). Second, the Germans have made the status of skilled worker coterminous with the completion of an apprenticeship. Thus Facharbeiter (skilled worker) is a legally protected status; you may only call yourself a Facharbeiter if you have passed the apprenticeship tests. This does not apply in Britain. Third, the Germans have not only expanded apprenticeship sideways, they have extended it downwards as well. That is, they have introduced semi or half-apprenticeships for some semi-skilled jobs, with codified training and syllabus(19). Note here the peculiarly German tendency to 'write-up' the skill element, rather than treat semi-skilled workers as interchangeable parts requiring only residual on-the-job training, as in Britain. Finally, apprenticeship is an important part of the process whereby employees qualify as foremen - which will be examined briefly in the next section.

But against the background of this contrast and overview, let us raise the question: in what sense may German managers be (in-part) qualified by virtue of the apprenticeship system? There are several answers.

The process for entering a Fachhochschule, outlined both in the discussion on engineering and economics, has not always been so. Until changes in the system in the early 1970s, the dominant mode of entry to the predecessor of the Fachhochschule was via a completed apprenticeship, followed by a short qualifying course (weeks not years) and so into the Fachhochschule. Thus, many older German managers who have the graduiert (supra) qualification in either technical or economic-business subjects began with an apprenticeship, which represented their first exposure to commerce or industry and constituted the first tranche of vocational training.

At an earlier point we noted that qualification levels on the commercial side of German companies tend to be lower than on the technical side. The practical implication is that there are many older generation middle managers in functions such as sales, marketing, costing, purchasing and, occasionally, personnel, who began their careers with a commercial apprenticeship (<u>Kaufmännische Lehre</u>) in industry and have acquired no further qualifications; this phenomenon preceded the rise of <u>Betriebswirtschaftslehre</u> described earlier.

A particular variation on this theme concerns banks. Banks offer their own apprenticeship (<u>Banklehre</u>) and, again, there is an older generation of section chiefs and bank managers for whom the apprenticeship is the only formal qualification, even if they will have benefited from various episodes of in-house training. The bank apprenticeships, incidentally, have come to be much sought after and applicants will generally have <u>Abitur</u> ('A' level GCE) rather than <u>mittlere Reife</u> ('O' level GCE), and it is said that there are ten times more applicants than there are available apprenticeship places.

Finally, because apprenticeship is something of a national institution, and at one with German values of practicality and vocationalism, it is quite common to find German managers who have done an apprenticeship because they wanted to and thought it would be instructive, even if it was not a necessary part of a qualification chain. This is facilitated by a shortening of the apprenticeship from three to two years for candidates who have <u>Abitur</u> at the start. It is not at all unusual to find business economics graduates who did an apprenticeship between school and university. Or to give a particular example, a survey of mechanical engineers in Germany in the late 1970s showed that a fifth of those with the Dipl.Ing. qualification, the university degree in engineering, had done an apprenticeship as well, although, of course, they did not have to(20)' A variation on this theme is the double apprenticeship;it is not uncommon for people in industry to do apprenticeships in two trades in quick succession - the author has met many such among the ranks of foremen and production managers, usually with the Ing.(grad.) qualification.

FOREMEN

Germany is one of the few countries in which there is a nationally standardised route and qualification set for becoming a foreman, and apprenticeship is the start.

The foreman in German is called <u>Meister</u> (master), and the implication is that he can exercise his craft in a <u>meisterlich</u> (masterly) fashion. The first step is an apprenticeship, with its successful completion conferring the legally protected status of <u>Facharbeiter</u> (skilled worker). Next follows several years of experience as a skilled workers and, then, on reaching the <u>age of 25, the aspiring foreman may enrol for a foreman's course.</u> The foreman's course is not a company phenomenon but a nationwide course administered by the same Industrie und Handelskammern (Chambers of Industry and Commerce) which control the apprenticeship system. The course can be done either full-time or part-time, but a part-time enrolment, spread over some 3 1/2 years, is normal. The course content tends to be technical rather than managerial, but not exclusively so: success in the examination at the end of the course leds to the granting of the <u>Meisterbrief</u> (foreman's certificate). The aspirant is then ready and qualified and may be appointed to a foreman's post when a suitable vacancy arises in his employing company.

It should be said that this is not the whole story. It is possible in Germany to promote to foreman posts people who lack the <u>Facharbeiter</u> and <u>Meisterbrief</u> qualifications described here. Such foremen are known as <u>Industrie-Meister</u> or <u>ernannte Werkmeister</u>, the connotation in both cases being one of 'conferred by industry', these unqualified foremen usually being found in areas of unskilled or semi-skilled work. The present writer has never seen figures on the relative numbers of qualified and unqualified foremen, and can only speak impressionistically; the impression is that the qualified foreman is the dominant type, professionally and numerically.

There are two further reasons for including this account of the foreman qualification system in a discussion of management training. There has been much discussion on both sides of the Atlantic on 'the problem of the first line supervisor', and it has been going on for nearly half a century(21). The essence of the perceived problem is that, traditionally, the foreman was a powerful figure, whose authority was equal to his tasks. But the advent of personnel officers and a lot of technical specialists deprived him of many of his functions - hiring and firing, setting pay, disciplining, job design, work control, scheduling, and so on.

Furthermore, the growth of trade union power and, especially, work-place employee representatives such as the shop stewards in Britain, have further limited his authority. A result has been that the foreman can scarcely cope with his remaining duties, lacks authority for their discharge, there is no competition to occupy the position and presenting-candidates tend not to be very high-powered.

Now the issue here is not to re-work a theme from Anglo-Saxon industrial sociology but to note that the German foreman system has largely by-passed the problem. The standing of the German foreman is based on his craft skill and technical knowledge, attained in two training courses and examinations. This is not something that personnel officers, production controllers, or works councillors (a very rough German equivalent to the British shop steward) can take away from him. So that, in the more explicitly technical milieu of the German factory, the foreman's authority is intact, his standing high and his powers adequate.

This leads us to the second consideration. In the English-speaking world, there is a lot of rhetoric about the foreman as the first level of management, although in practice it tends not to amount to very much. In Britain, certainly, the average foreman has more in common with those he supervises, educationally and socio-culturally, than with the managers above him, whose privileges he does not usually share.

Although the rhetoric is missing there is more substance to the claim in West Germany. Better educated, better qualified, technically more independent foremen are able to do more for their management supervisors, discharging some of the functions that in, say Britain, would be the province of the production superintendent.(22)

IN THE COMPANIES

It was suggested at an earlier stage that in-company training in Germany is important and occurs on a significant scale. This is true, it is consistent with German values of practicality and specificity, and it goes with some of the _lacunae_ noted at the outset - no MBAs, business schools, and so on.

There is, however, a certain difficulty about 'laying bare' this aspect of management training in

Germany; this is that it is happening in private industry, not in the public domain. Companies are not secretive about their training programs, the author has had many discussions with representatives of German companies, but the German corporate in-house training totality is not something that one can go away and look up in the public library! This makes generalisations more difficult - but not impossible.

First, it is desirable to underline the simple importance of in-company training in Germany; there is a good deal of it, it is taken seriously and the organisation of training constitutes a larger part of the personnel function in Germany than in say Britain.(23) Second, in the period of the author's own interest in German management there does seem to have been a gentle trend away from the exclusively technical and towards the specifically managerial. Third, for the most part, the management content of such in-company programs does tend towards the specific rather than the general; for example courses on management by objectives, problem-solving techniques, goal-setting, and so on, have become common. Fourth, courses tend to be designed to meet specific needs: courses for newly appointed foremen (going beyond the Meisterbrief) for instance, or courses for section chiefs on staff appraisal. Fifth, the in-company course offering tends to be targeted as to those attending them, not only by need but by audience homogeneity. People attending a course organised by a German company will be from the same function - sales, production, design or whatever, and be of the same approximate hierarchical level.

Some of these characterising points can be made the other way round by noting some things that German corporate training does not do. It is less used as a reward for good performance than in the USA or Britain ('he's the best on the section, send him on the xyz course - it'll give him a week in London'). The German course system is also less used to flag official approval and imminent promotion; it is need-driven, rather than status or reward-driven.

Finally, there is another contrast. The Anglo-Saxon idea that trainees will benefit from a heterogeneous association with people from other types of jobs, organisations, and perhaps even branches of industry, that more will be gained from multifarious exposure, rubbing shoulders, making contacts, than from the formal content of the course, does not inform German thinking on corporate training. This would be a violation of the German understanding of vocational specifics.

GENERAL MANAGEMENT AT LAST?

To complete this survey of the ways and means by which German managers are trained and educated it should be said that there is a miscellany of non-profit making organisations offering management courses. These are outside both the state education system, on the one hand, and the training enterprise of single companies, on the other. These organisations are loosely federated into what is called the Wuppertaler Kreis (Wuppertal circle) and the courses do take people from a variety of companies and other employing organisations.

Now to continue a leitmotiv of this account, even some of these are specific as to content or clientele. The Rationalisierungs-Kuratorium der deutschen Wirtschaft (RTW, German productivity council), for instance, is concerned with rationa-lisation and industrial efficiency matters rather than with the range of management performance. Or again,the Junge Untermekmer der Arbeitsgemeinschaft Selbeständiger Untermehmer (young entrepreneurs section of the independent entrepreneurs' associa-tion), by definition, has a specialist clientele with distinctive economic interests.

But the bulk of the courses alluded to here are general, in a way that little else on the German management training scene is. The most famous of these is the Baden-Baden Untermehmergespräch (Baden-Baden management conference). Founded in the early 1950s, very prestigious and select, aimed at managers on or just about to join the Vorstand (the executive board of the publicly-quoted AG type companies), it gives delegates three weeks of graceful association and a diffuse socialisation in the responsibilities of business. Delegates are, of course, drawn from a variety of companies, and have progressed beyond purely functional management responsibilities.

The Berliner Institut für Befriebsführung (Berlin business management institute) and the Rudolf Poensgen Stiftung (foundation), to cite two others, have a similar generalist approach, with lectures on a variety of management functions for all delegates, and there are several other organisations offering courses of this ilk.

So West Germany does provide some general management education, after all. But it is for the few rather than the many, of short rather than long duration. And the customers are no longer in the first flush of youth but managers already qualified and specialised as engineers, business economists, chemists and lawyers.

END THOUGHTS

Germany is a remarkable country. Both in management style and in the provision of education for managers it is conspicuously self-sufficient (and immune to American influence). Far more so than, say, France, which is popularly credited with a strong sense of idiosyncratic nationalism.

This is more remarkable given the turmoil and vicissitudes of Germany in the twentieth century - defeat in two world wars, the horrors and subsequent moral burden of Nazism, military occupation, loss of territory and division. Much has changed, but those issues which are the concerns of this chapter have probably changed least in the last forty years. An important part of the explanation for this is that West Germany has enjoyed a remarkable level of economic success since the post-war recovery.(24) Germany has also been good at surviving the vicissitudes - the 1973-74 oil crisis, the run-away inflation of the mid-1970s, the 1979 oil shock, the world recession and mounting unemployment of the 1980s. All these have affected West Germany, yet that country has survived better than most.

So the interesting questions are: will Germany change, should Germany change, and what would make it change?

NOTES

1. P. Lawrence, 'Management in the Netherlands: A Study in Internationalism?, Report for the Technische Hogeschool Twente, Enschede, Netherlands (1986).

2. Booz, Allen & Hamilton Report, English Translation, 'German Management', International Studies of Management and Organisation, Arts & Science Press Inc. (Spring/Summer 1973).

3. C. Handy, et al, The Making of Managers, Economic Development Office, London (1987).

4. P.A. Lawrence, Managers and Management in West Germany, Croom Helm, London (1980).

5. Ibid.

6. J.H. Horovitz, Top Management Control in Europe, MacMillan, London (1980).

7. A. Sorge & W. Warner, Comparative Factory Organisation, Gower Publishing Company, Aldershot, England (1986).

8. S.P. Hutton & P.A. Lawrence, German Engineers: Anatomy of a Profession, Oxford University Press, Oxford (1981).

9. C.P. Snow, 'The Two Cultures and the Scientific Revolution', The Rede Lecture (1959).

10. B. May, Social, Educational and Professional Background of German Management, Report to the Department of Industry, London (1974).

11. G. Brinkmann, 'Die Ausbilding für Führungskräften für die Wirtschaft', Üniversitätsverlag Michael Wienand, Cologne (1967).

12. H. Bayer & P. Lawrence, 'Engineering Education and the Status of Industry', European Journal of Engineering Education, No.2 (1977).

13. S.P. Hutton, P.A. Lawrence & J.H. Smith, The Recruitment, Development and Status of the Mechanical Engineer in the German Federal Republic, Report to the Department of Industry, London (1977).

14. P.A. Lawrence, Personnel Management in West Germany: Portrait of a Function, Report to the International Institute of Management, West Berlin (1982).

15. G. Brinkmann, 'Die Ausbilding für Führungskräften für die Wirtschaft', Üniversitätsverlag Michael Wienand, Cologne (1967).

16. R.R. Locke, The End of Practical Man, JAI Press Incorporated, Greenwich, Connecticut & London, England (1984).

17. A. Sorge & W. Warner, Comparative Factory Organisation, Gower Publishing Company, Aldershot, England (1986).

18. K. Wagner, Relation between Education, Employment and Productivity and their Impact on Education and Labour Market Policies: A British-German Comparison, Report for the European Centre for the Development of Vocational Training, Berlin (1983).

19. A. Sorge & M. Warner, Manpower Training, Manufacturing Organisation and Work Roles in Great Britain and West Germany, Discussion Paper 78-96 of the International Institute of Management, West Berlin, December (1978).

20. S.P. Hutton, P.A. Lawrence & J.H. Smith, The Recruitment, Development and Status of the Mechanical Engineer in the German Federal Republic, Report to the Department of Industry, London (1977).

21. F.J. Roethlisberger, 'The Foreman: Master and Victim of Double Talk', Harvard Business Review (1945).

22. M. Fores, P. Lawrence & A. Sorge, 'Germany's Front Line Force', Management Today, (March 1978).

23. P.A. Lawrence, Personnel Management in West Germany: Portrait of a Function, Report to the International Institute of Management, West Berlin (1982).

24. P.A. Lawrence, Managers and Management in West Germany, Croom Helm, London (1980).

Chapter Eight

MANAGEMENT EDUCATION IN JAPAN
Kevin Collins

Japan's modernisation and industrialisation did not
really commence until the Meiji Restoration in
1868.   Prior to this, a cottage industry and
domestic factory system had developed through the
efforts of indigenous entrepreneurs, and the
Tokugawa Shogunate (1603-1867) belatedly realising
the perils of the policy of isolation initiated
over two hundred years previously, had sought Dutch
assistance to establish modern steel works and
shipyards in 1859.   After sending missions extensively through Western industrialised countries,
the process of transforming the traditional feudal
society into a modern nation commenced. Instructors
and experts in various fields were brought to Japan
both to initiate the introduction of the new technology and to train Japanese workers to operate the
new systems.   The nature and extent of foreign
influence is indicated by Dickerman.

> 'Commercial banking and cotton spinning
> were strongly influenced by English
> experts, as was the architecture of many
> of the buildings. The French and Scotch
> built the first shipyards and a French
> engineer designed the first mechanized
> silk thread factory. Porcelain manufac-
> turing and the chemical industries were
> developed by German experts. The French
> influenced civil law and the Germans,
> public law and the constitution. Accoun-
> ting systems came primarily from the
> Germans. After the publication of Taylor's

Scientific Management, the influence of
the American management methods became
stronger in Japan, and much emphasis was
placed on efficiency'.(1)

Allowing for the surprising omission of the
American, then German influence on the national
system of education which prepared the population
for both modernisation, and later, militarism, the
above suggests how widely Japan had spread its
search for foreign technology. From this point on,
Japan used education to shape the attitudes,
behaviour and skills of its population to prepare
the large numbers of workers, scientists, leaders
and entrepreneurs needed for industrial and
military strength.

INDUSTRIAL STRUCTURE AND MANAGEMENT NEEDS

During the first major drive for industrialisation
between 1890 and 1912, it was estimated that the
national income more than tripled(2). While secondary industry had only contributed approximately 16
per cent of this in 1890, by 1912 its contribution
had grown to more than 25 per cent. Between 1868
and 1890 the government was involved directly with
some economic enterprises, but changed from state
entrepreneurship to cooperation with private
enterprise by selling off the factories to selected
recipients. Through a combination of formal and
informal patronage the government nurtured these
early modern businesses and, in return, expected
them to carry out its policy of expansion and
development. Other factors in addition to government patronage were also required for development
to occur. These being accumulation of capital, an
efficient labour source, and effective leadership.
Fortunately, Japan was able to benefit from an
accumulated fund of domestic savings resulting from
a tradition of frugality and diligence, a large
pool of skilled artisans who quickly learned the
skills of the new technology, and the considerable
administrative expertise of a large body of
educated samurai who took over the mantle of
leadership in various fields.(3)
    The rate of industrialisation and economic
development progressed steadily, with successes in
the Sino-Japanese and Russo-Japanese Wars not only
resulting from and restimulating industrial growth,
but also unifying the population in a belief in

Japan's economic and military parity with the Western nations. Utilising an extremely effective educational system to shape the attitudes and behaviour of the population to diligently seek for greater national prosperity and military power by self sacrifice and self discipline, Japan marched steadily towards international parity in industry and to its eventual defeat in World War II through its nationalism and militarism.

When the Occupation Forces entered Japan they had two main objectives - to prevent Japan from having the capacity to wage war, and to create an economic and social climate conducive to democracy. A fourfold plan was developed to achieve this:

a) dissolve the zaibatsu, the powerful industrial and financial cliques such as Mitsubishi, Mitsui, Sumitomo and Yamaha
b) break up the high concentration in key industries
c) purge senior executives in major firms, and
d) pass an Anti-Monopoly Law.

These objectives were only partially attained and many of the achievements that were made have since been overturned. Family ownership and control of the zaibatsu were removed, the holding companies dissolved, and subsidiary companies became independent. Since then, however, the shortage of funds during the reconstruction period caused the former zaibatsu companies to seek funds from previously affiliated firms and banks and to gradually re-establish ties. This was further assisted by two revisions of the Anti-Monopoly Act in 1949 and 1953, resulting in a steady increase in cross-holdings of stock between firms previously connected in a zaibatsu. In later years these zaibatsu again reformed with the three major pre-war zaibatsu Sumitomo, Mitsui and Mitsubishi being the first to establish coordinating councils which met regularly. These new groups, each with its own bank, are now well diversified and very influential. Only limited success was achieved in the Occupation attempts to break up the concentration in key industries. Out of a total of 325 large firms targeted, only 11 were dissolved, due to the important role they played in the early postwar economy. The Japanese government had traditionally been supportive of big business since early in the Meiji era, and they subtly but persistently resisted the attempts of SCAP (General Douglas

MacArthur, Supreme Commander for the Allied Powers) to both break down the zaibatsu and to reduce the concentration of large firms. The government also channelled large amounts of capital to those enterprises engaged in such key industries as ship building, iron and steel in an attempt to boost the rate of reconstruction. The net result of these activities was that 'the structure and organisation of the large Japanese enterprises, though their physical assets were destroyed and their senior executive purged, remained virtually unaltered'.(4) The reforms of the occupation era were significant, however, in that they helped modernise the zaibatsu by freeing them from earlier family domination, increasing their number and promoting the development of labour unions.

The year 1952 saw the economy regain its prewar output, and the end of the American Occupation. Between 1951 and 1963 real national output had nearly tripled, and was growing at over 9 per cent per year. Per capita income grew at an average of 8 per cent per year, and had doubled during this 13 year period. Manufacturing had increased fivefold and exports had nearly doubled. Agriculture, forestry and fishing, while decreasing in national economic importance not only increased by approximately 50 per cent but, due to the process of mechanisation, needed less labour, thus releasing half a million workers to provide labour for the new industrial developments.(5)

During the later postwar years there has been little public ownership of industry. While such essential services as the telephone and telegraph industry, and the nation's key railroad network have had government ownership, these are now being sold to private interests. Once again economic power has become concentrated between a relatively small number of firms with key industries such as iron and steel, shipbuilding, and oil refining now totally in the private sector. Small and medium size firms continue to be an important source of employment and income as they employ approximately two thirds of the workforce. The relationship of industrial dualism present in the prewar period thus still persists, with the larger, modern, capital-intensive, technologically oriented enterprises coexisting with the traditional sector comprised mainly of small businesses and workshops.

Government, while moving away from direct involvement, still plays a role in industrial growth and development. Although it does not normally give direct orders to businesses, it does reward those businesses that listen to its suggestions or hints by providing easy access to capital, giving them tax breaks, and approving plans to import foreign technology. This is normally done through the offices of the Ministry of International Trade and Industry (MITI). Such a relationship was very important in the period of high speed growth when control of foreign exchange virtually meant control of economic growth and development. Foreign currency allocations were dispersed by MITI, and were used to implement industrial policy. The foreign exchange budget existed as early as the 1880s, appeared again in 1937, and persisted in one form or other until 1964. Not only was MITI felt to be the main source of inspiration and movement towards heavy and chemical industries but more recently, has been actively involved in 'supporting' consortium formation to research development of the micro-chip industry. Johnson summarises what MITI believes to be its main achievement by quoting from Ohkawa and Rosovsky.

> 'In the first half of the 1950s approximately 30 per cent of exports still consisted of fibres and textiles, and another 20 per cent was classified as sundries. Only 14 per cent was in the category of machinery. By the first half of the 1960s, after the great investment spurt, major changes in composition had taken place. Fibres and textiles were down to 8 per cent and sundries 14 per cent, and machinery with 30 per cent had assumed its position of leading component, followed by metals and metal products (26 per cent)'.(6)

THE NEEDS OF INDUSTRY IN MANAGEMENT EDUCATION

Management practices followed by successful merchants during the Tokugawa period were based on the family. The merchant house would take in apprentices, and over a period of many years the latter would increase their skills as they worked in the household of the merchant. During this period they were treated as part of the extended family, even to the point that when they left they could establish a branch house, in many cases with financial help from the head house. This simulated kinship, or familialism was utilised at various times during the modernisation of Japan in an attempt to cope with labour-unrest, and to establish loyalty and stability in the workforce. The introduction of modern technology and methods of production found the vast majority of merchants totally incapable of coping. Even prominent merchant houses such as Mitsui only survived through the ability of its younger, more flexible members.

As more technology was introduced it became necessary to have a well trained, skilled, stable workforce. In an effort to retain workers, employers began to pay much more attention to employees' needs. This led to the introduction of the paternalistic approach characterised by such features as lifetime employment and a seniority-based reward system, as management became more involved in workers' lives. Realising that the family system represented the core of traditional Japanese values, and that 'ideal' family attributes were even emphasised by governmental presentation of the nation as a family with the Emperor as head, even the zaibatsu structured themselves on this pattern and reinforced the concept by giving tangible 'family' benefits to employees.

Japan's defeat in World War II, and the separation of owners from the various zaibatsu and large firms resulted in managerial openings appearing for younger men. Many of these men had graduated from tertiary institutions in the 1920s or early 1930s and were employed in middle management during the 1940s.

> In a 1966 survey of presidents of 1150 major companies listed in the Tokyo Stock Exchange it was found that 88 per cent had attended universities and approximately 27 per cent were graduates of Tokyo University. Other public universities such as Kyoto, Hitotsubashi, Kobe and Tokyo Technical accounted for another 30 per cent and 13 per cent were graduates of Keio and Waseda Universities, both of which are private'.(7)

With the tight governmental regulations and control from holding companies removed, the new managers had more freedom to try new managerial methods.

Since the war, industry has looked to its management to provide stability in periods of chaos in those years of reconstruction immediately following the war, and in the fluctuating periods of growth

and change up to the present day. Labour unrest,
the search for new technology, and increased
productivity and profitability presented management
with constant challenges. While many enterprises
persisted with paternalistic practices based on
lifetime employment, seniority-based salary and
extensive fringe benefits, others looked to management to propose different solutions based on a
reform or revision of capitalism. One such proposal
came from a group called the Keizai Doyukai, which
was formed by a group of young, progressive
executives in 1946.(8) In 1947 this group released
a proposal calling for professional managers to
assume the role of mediators to bring harmony
between workers and shareholders, and establish a
'tripartite, democratic, cooperative entity of
management, capital and labor'.(9) Strong
opposition to this proposal came from management,
which did not wish to alter their existing pattern,
and labour which 'was espousing socialism'. The
Doyukai put forward another major proposal in 1956
which urged, for the creation of a climate of fair
competition, the removal of monopolies, a more
equal distribution of corporate earnings, and
emphasised the 'need for improvement of managerial
practices and the training of future generations of
managers' by 'systematic efforts in management
development'.(10) An interesting point to note here
is that this proposal was made following the Japan
Productivity Centre-sponsored visit of a group of
top management personnel to America, which was the
first visit of such a group. The Doyukai proposal
was similar to, and felt to be influenced by, the
then current American managerial ideology, and was
considered to be the Japanese version of American
managerial philosophy.

Between the late 1950s and the 1960s Japan went
through a period of very rapid growth which
encouraged business to further expand and diversify. The business community responded to this so
successfully that, by the early 1960s, they had not
only caught up with demand but found that their
excess capacity led to fierce competition. It was
not long before some companies experienced a downturn in profitability and started laying-off temporary workers and contractors. Business leaders
became disillusioned with their inability to be
able to follow the social responsibility expectations framed in the American-influenced Doyukai
proposal and began to search for a more appropriate
Japanese philosophy. A response came once again

from the Doyukai. In 1965 it published a statement which was critical of the traditional feature of Japanese management, paternalism, and stressed that managerial policy should emphasise functionalism, flexibility and professionalism. The statement also argued that pursuing profit in a legitimate and responsible manner was vital for corporate success and would need managers to develop their abilities as innovators, leaders, and promoters of economic growth.(11) Despite this proposal, and indications that paternalism is losing its appeal for employees, a large proportion of management still follow the traditional paternalistic practices. With the cost of maintaining these practices continually rising, those committed to them may, out of necessity, be forced to abandon them.

Should this occur, what new approach will be followed? Traditionally, Japanese business leaders, like their Western counterparts, have managed through groups. The extent of group organisation, group-oriented behaviour and group activity in Japan, however, is much greater than that found in other countries and is deliberately fostered. So great an emphasis has been placed on group-oriented behaviour by Japanese employers/ managers, that governmental guidelines have been laid down for elementary and secondary school teachers to ensure that a large proportion of future employees are shaped in this way. While industry continues to operate on group-based activities and all levels of society and education cultivate and reinforce group-oriented behaviour, then Japanese style management will continue. If, as current trends might appear to indicate, group orientation gives way to a greater degree of individualism, what approach will industry and management follow to retain industrial and national prosperity? With the current and future changes in the managerial environment, managerial attributes must emphasise flexibility so that industry can cope with societal and economic change.

A study tour of American and European institutions by a group of Japanese training personnel and executives in 1973 brought forward several interesting reactions. The tour was run jointly by the International Management Association of Japan in association with Time-Life Educational systems, and the group of twenty-one visited fifteen business schools and institutions in five European countries as well as North America over a twenty-four day period. One general point mentioned was that the

employment structure in Western nations was different from that found in Japan, where loyalty to the
company, lifetime employment and the seniority
system of rewards tended to keep stability in the
workforce. As a result, the selection and training
of managerial personnel can be done gradually over
a period of years. The greater mobility of staff,
including managerial personnel, in Western countries was both an indication of, and resulted in,
much lower sense of loyalty to the company. In a
situation such as this, it becomes more important
to obtain capable managers who have already gained
their training through an outside institution. The
comments, which tended to fall into one of three
basic views could be characterised by the
following:

A.   '... it is imperative that Japan have more
     business executives of international calibre to
     keep abreast with the rest of the world. Toward
     this end, the need is keenly felt to send more
     and more of our talented executives for further
     training at leading business schools in Europe
     and the US'. (Quote by Personnel Manager,
     Mitsubishi Bank).

B.   'In the light of the uniquely Japanese employ-
     ment practice that is predicated upon life-time
     tenure and seniority system, it is quite natu-
     ral that the emphasis of managerial education
     has been on the training of executives to fit
     into the various levels of individual corpora-
     tions' management structure, rather than on the
     development of Western-type professional
     managers with industry-wide acceptability ...
     If so, unless the entire personnel administra-
     tion system of Japanese corporations including
     their managerial education and promotion
     programs is fundamentally revamped, it appears
     doubtful if the purpose of developing
     international-minded managers can be fully
     served by sending trainees to these Western
     business schools. Perhaps it is time for us to
     start giving serious consideration to the task
     of establishing our own managerial education
     centres that are specially tailored to the
     needs of Japanese businesses'. (Quote from
     Personnel Manager, Hattori and Co. Ltd.).

C.   'What I saw in Europe and the US made me keenly
     aware of the urgent need for managerial

education in Japan to be raised in both scope and quality to a level comparable to that in the West, but at the same time, it was reassuring to find that the Japanese management practice had many merits of its own that should be retained and promoted'.(Quote from Personnel Manager, Industrial Bank of Japan).(12)

From these statements it would appear that the categories into which the views of those in the tour held would be as follows:

A.   Japan should quickly copy, or send trainees to, Western managerial programs.

B.   Japan is a different culture and needs its own programs based on Japanese business needs and characteristics.

C.   Japan should establish business schools of its own which combine the best from both Japanese and Western managerial programs.

An interesting point to note is that two themes appeared regularly in the reports of the tour members. The first of these was the necessity for close co-operation between industry and academic institutions when developing managerial programs, and the second was the virtually unanimous acceptance of the need for specialised managerial education programs to be introduced in Japanese academic institutions to aid in the development of managerial personnel. As will be seen later, the people in the managerial hierarchy in many Japanese companies do not necessarily agree that training outside the company is an advantage.

BEGINNING OF MANAGEMENT EDUCATION

Management education in many forms and from various sources sprang into being to assist Japanese indus-try and enterprises. These programs, as distinct from the day to day on-the-job training given within industry, were normally geared to the needs of current managerial personnel - whether junior, middle, or top management - or to those being considered for such roles. As indicated in the survey of presidents of major companies mentioned earlier, as early as 1966 the vast majority (88 per cent) had completed tertiary education prior to joining the company. It should be noted that where mention has been made about such aspects as life-time employment within companies, that this refers in the main to large companies, and that a policy of this nature is maintained by employing other workers on temporary-basis, subcontracting work out to small companies, or a combination of both. In this way, when it becomes necessary to reduce production due to, for example, a drop in sales, those with lifetime employment remain secure, while temporary employees and/or employees in the subcon-tracting or small affiliated companies are laid off. Many middle-sized companies have attempted to copy some of the practices followed by larger companies, and the attainment of a university education as a basic requirement for consideration for management would be common to both.

The actual content of the tertiary courses is not of great significance to future employers, as it would be extremely difficult to design a course or program which met the extremely diverse and practical needs of each possible employer. In addition to this, Japanese universities have tended to emphasise 'philosophical thinking and training in theoretical principles rather than technical and practical education and training in specific subjects'.(13) Most companies tend to consider that courses at secondary and tertiary institutions are far too abstract and lacking in practical content to be of any real value and, instead, look to these institutions to develop desirable patterns of behaviour and attitudes to work. They also consider the hierarchical status of the institution from which the applicant graduated, as this is felt to be not only a guide to the ability of the applicant, but also that the 'old-boy' network among tertiary graduates might prove useful to the company in the years ahead. Thus each graduate who enters a company is considered to have a general, rather than a specialist, education and has the potential to be trained for management. During the early years they are rotated between the various branches or sectors of the enterprise to develop their knowledge, skill and experience in all aspects of the company's operations and to determine their possible managerial potential. To this end the technical training they receive is not intended to make them competent technicians, but rather to give them a broad general background as preparation for a managerial position.

182

Managerial training in Japan can be provided within the enterprise, by attendance at a variety of specialised institutions which run programs for the various aspects and levels of management, and by degree or diploma granting universities. In the period up to 1945, management training was almost exclusively carried out within the company and was basically on-the-job training gained as those being considered were given a variety of experiences and opportunities to demonstrate their ability. As will be seen in the chronological summary which follows, the first efforts by outside organisations began in the 1940s, gradually increasing in range as the demand grew and the number of training bodies increased.

1942:   Japanese Efficiency School
- Offered courses in efficiency, office management, cost accounting, personnel management, production control.

1945:   Japanese Standards Association
- Private organisation, but with government and business sponsorship.
- Courses offered: Quality control and standardisation.
- 25 day courses for middle managers in manufacturing.
- full time course once or twice a year in each of seven cities.

1947:   US Occupation Forces (Civil Communications Section) Programs
- Introduced a series of programs developed in the United States during World War II.
- Courses offered: Training Within Industry (TWI), Middle Management Training Program (MTP).
- Courses offered to supervisory personnel and were widely adopted by large and small Japanese firms.

1950:   Institute of Business Administration (IBAM)
- Grew out of the Japanese Efficiency School.
- Continued offering courses as in Japanese Efficiency School.
- 1965 it began a series of Managerial Grid courses.

- Courses offered include: sensitivity training, management grid seminars, computer utilisation, and more than 25 diversified management courses.

NOTE: See SANNO. In 1979 IBAM was renamed SANNO Institute of Business Administration.

1950s: Japan Management Association
- Courses introduced to deal with problems of industrial engineering and related functions.
- 1955 Inventory control course.
- 1958 Preventive maintenance course.
- 1959 Production control course.
- 1963 Courses on market research application.
- Top management course, sales management course.
- Office management.

1953: Central Japan Industries Association
- Formed to offer management consulting services to its members.
- Central Japan Institute of Industrial Management is an affiliate and offers courses to supervisory and management personnel.
- 1966 Junior Executive Academy inaugurated - 1 year full time course for young men being trained to take over top management in family business.

1953: Japan Productivity Centre
- Established in cooperation with US Government
- Offers a variety of programs throughout Japan
- Courses offered include: managerial economics, decision making, management information, personnel administration and industrial relations.
- Courses run for different periods, and for different levels.

1956: Keio University Managerial Program
- Western top management concepts introduced at Keio, when the Keio-Harvard Advanced Management Program was initiated.
- Faculty initially from Harvard, now Harvard trained Japanese faculty plus visiting Harvard faculty.

- Courses offered: Advanced management, management development seminar, junior management development seminar.

1961: <u>Asian Productivity Organisation</u>
- Established with headquarters in Japan.
- Aim: Increase productivity in member Asian countries such as Hong Kong, India, Sri Lanka, Indonesia, Pakistan by concerted productivity drive and cooperation.
- Courses offered: once a year course called Small Business Management Trainers and Consultants Training Course.

1965: <u>Academy of Management Development</u>
- Established by Japan Productivity Centre.
- Aim: Introduce modern techniques from the United States and Europe.
- Courses offered include: marketing, production management, financial management, systems and computer.

1967: <u>Sophia University</u>
- International Division of the School of Business began a Master's program in International Business and Management.
- Courses conducted in English for young Japanese executives wishing to develop ability to become international businessmen.
- Courses are supplemented by International Development Seminars run by its Socio-Economic Institute.
- Courses offered include: finance, marketing, personnel, government relations, and joint ventures.

1968: <u>Japan Institute of Business Administration</u>
- A division of the Japan Management School.
- Management development program.
- Courses offered include: personnel training, labour relations and general management.

1969: <u>Keio University</u>
- Inaugurated a 2 year Master of Business Administration Program based on the Harvard University program.
- 1978 the Graduate School of Business Administration was formally established.

1969: <u>Institute of International Studies and Training</u>
- Established by a special act of Parliament and supervised by MITI.
- Graduate level training.
- Board of directors selected from government, business and educational institutions.
- Courses offered include: Intensive English language, area studies of selected countries, international business, and includes a one week tour of Japan and one month tour abroad in selected area of concentration.

1973: <u>University of Tsukuba: Graduate Division</u>
- Two year full-time program in management.

NOTE: Many universities now offer undergraduate programs in business administration. In 1981 Sasaki commented that 62 out of the total of 389 colleges and universities had departments in this area of study. Because of (a) the large number involved, and (b) the fact that the undergraduate courses are aimed at young students who are mostly inexperienced in the work force, no further mention will be made of them.

1979: <u>Sanno Management School</u>
- An offshoot of Sanno Institute of Business Administration which originated in 1950.
- One year program for potential managers with a first degree.
- Was originally called the Institute of Business Administration and Management.
- Courses offered: See IBAM.
  Also runs the Entrepreneur Development Training Scheme for Malaysian Businessmen (sponsored by the Malaysian government), an International Seminar on Japanese Business and Management, and an Executive Development Program for foreign managers of subsidiaries in Japan.

1982: <u>International University of Japan: Graduate School</u>
- Two year Master's program.
- Courses offered include: A variety of courses within such general groupings as International Politics, International Economics, International Management,

Japanese Studies, North American Studies, East and Southeast Asian Studies, Middle Eastern Studies.

NOTE: Comprehensive listings and information are not available. This chronology was compiled from information presented in the two world surveys of McNulty 1969 and 1980,(14) publications by Dickerman and Subocz,(15) and from brochures/handbooks from some of the institutions.

TRAINING WITHIN THE ENTERPRISE

While extensive training programs had been developed by many companies for the normal rank and file workers in the pre-war period, very little attention had been given to providing formal programs for potential or current managerial personnel. Whether this was due to the influence of the 'merchant house' system which, according to Clark(16) had a continuing effect on the 'industrial organisation of Japan', or whether the generally paternalistic philosophy of the company was echoed in the expectation that potential managers would develop through their work experiences, it is difficult to say. Other aspects of the pre-Meiji 'merchant house' system were adopted during this period, however, and to a certain extent still exist today i.e. lifetime employment, and simulated familial relations within the company.

In the early post-war period there were few courses on management run by tertiary institutions or management associations, and little or no contact between industry and educational institutions. Most private companies felt that such essential managerial characteristics as a 'broad range of intellectual capability, decision-making ability and leadership, ... were best developed through empirical means, while working'.(17) As Japan's production was mostly directed at the domestic market at this stage, it was generally felt that it was best to continue with the procedures and conduct which had been followed previously where training was given through job rotation and occasional instruction given by superiors. At this stage the Training Within Industry (TWI) and the Middle Management Training Program (MTP) initiated by the Occupation Forces was introduced and gradually gained support.

Rapid postwar growth brought many problems with it, problems which many firms felt might be overcome with the help of TWI and MTP. Not only were many companies growing quickly in size and complexity, but the rapid rate of change was of great concern to management. New positions were created, with new skills to be given to existing personnel through training. The two programs were adopted widely among Japanese companies, with one leading firm, for example, having '350 qualified TWI trainers on its staff'.(18) While the chronology indicates that specialised, professional organisations began to offer more management education activities outside the enterprises, universities had not responded in a manner felt to be of value by industry as is indicated by a comment by Yoshino:

> 'Typically, university training in business management has been quite general and has not been geared to the practical needs of corporations. Moreover, (in 1968) there is no program in Japanese universities equivalent to the Master of Business Administration degree program found in many American universities. It is up to individual firms to train their new recruits from the universities in specific skills relating to various aspects of management'.(19)

A survey of 683 company presidents concerning top management development programs, conducted by the Tokyo Chamber of Commerce in 1970, indicated that few companies had in-house training programs for this group. The survey also reported that the vast majority of those interviewed felt that graduate schools of business were needed.(20)

THE PRESENT SITUATION

A quick perusal of the chronology presented earlier would indicate the number and diversity of managerial programs offered by various institutions which have been developed in the postwar period. The fact that this list is far from comprehensive in that it does not include all the universities which now offer graduate and undergraduate programs in business administration, or the smaller educational bodies offering managerial courses, quickly makes it very clear that it would not be possible (even if desirable) to discuss them all in the space available. Subocz,(21) when commenting on the increase in popularity of these courses, said that, of the approximately 300 separate institutes operating in the early 1960s, as many as 200 'seminar organisers' still existed in the 1980s. With this in mind, a careful selection of both institutional programs and in-house programs will be discussed in an attempt to present an accurate picture of current practices in Japan.

Japan Productivity Centre

This Centre is a private, non-profit organisation which was established in cooperation with the United States government in the early postwar years. In 1965, an Academy of Management Development was established and modern techniques from Europe and America were introduced through its programs. A variety of courses are offered to particular levels of management and certificates are awarded upon successful completion of the course. The aim of this Academy was 'to meet the need for a more formal approach toward intensified education, as achieved by the Harvard Business School'.(22) Courses deal with the latest theories of business management and administration as well as their practical application, cultivating the individual's speciality, encouraging the intellectual creativity necessary to cope and adapt to change, and to provide a good grounding for leadership roles. To ensure that the courses and course content meet the needs of industry, liaison conferences are held from time to time to exchange views and ideas with company officials. In 1987, ten one-year courses were available, which operated one full-day a week. The methods used usually combined lectures with group study and discussion, with a report to be presented at the end of the year. Each course commenced in April and ended in March of the following year. A list of courses offered and numbers enrolled in 1987 follows:

Course	No.	Level of Participant
Top Management Course	49	Top management
International course	27	Open
Management Decision-Making Course	47	Middle Management
Human Ability & Organisational Development course	33	Middle "
Marketing Course	64	Junior "
Production Management Course	34	" "
Management Finance Course	39	" "
Personnel Administration Course	40	" "
Managerial Economics Course	29	Middle "
Computer Management Course	31	" "
	___	
TOTAL	391	
	___	

In addition to the Academy programs mentioned above three to four day seminars were run 'outside' the Academy by the Japan Productivity Centre for top management personnel. The seminars which were run by a combination of government officials, business executives and academics dealt with such topics as politics, economics, and social and international relations aspects which could affect their business. These courses were designed for both new and prospective managers. Other short seminars and courses (one to ten days) covered such areas as personnel administration, marketing, finance, and corporate planning. Approximately 170 seminars of this type are run annually.

Keio University: Graduate School of Business Administration

The school was established in 1978 to develop professional managers, and is claimed to be the closest equivalent to the MBA qualification found in western countries. Origins of this program can be traced back to 1956 when western managerial concepts were introduced at Keio through the introduction of the Keio-Harvard Management Program. In 1962 Keio Business School was founded, and has been offering various types of courses on business management in the form of short-term seminars and a one-year non-degree program since then. By 1969,

Keio decided to establish a more extensive and comprehensive program and introduced the Master of Business Administration which is a two year full-time program. Divided into five semesters, the curriculum consists of eleven core courses and at least five elective courses.

Core Courses

Human Behaviour in
  Organisations
Data Processing Systems
Managerial Economics
Accounting
Production Policy
International Business

Marketing
Finance
Human Resource Management
Business Environment
Business Policy

The electives may be drawn from a wide range which currently covers more than forty courses associated with the core topics, but mostly at an advanced level. The case method is used as the primary method of teaching. This approach involves individual study, group discussion and class discussion.

Keio Business School also provides courses for present and potential managers. Currently the school offers five seminars on business management.

Management Development Seminar	- 3 months
Advanced Management Seminar	- 10 days
Middle Management Seminar	- 2 weeks
Junior Management Seminar	- 2 weeks
The Distribution Seminar	- 6 days

Sanno Institute of Business Administration (SIBA)

Founded in 1950, SANNO is one of the largest private organisations in the field of management development in Japan. This Institute is the culmination of two previous schools, the first being the Japanese Efficiency School which eventually developed into the Institute of Business Administration (IBAM) in 1950. Yoichi Ueno founded both the early schools and, after his death in 1957, his son took over as chairman. In 1979 the IBAM was renamed the SANNO Institute of Business Administration, and the SANNO Management School (SMS) was established in the same year. SMS offers courses which run from April to October inclusive, with participants drawn from the same level of management. The participants come together on 14 days - twice a month - for full day group seminars, and do individual research between group meetings. Certificates are awarded upon successful completion of the course.

Courses

1. Business Strategy
2. Marketing A (Staff)
3. Marketing B (Line)
4. Overseas Expansion
5. Profit Strategy
6. Production Control Systems
7. Personnel Affairs
8. Education Programs
9. Future Technology

The SIBA runs a variety of business consulting services, in-company training programs, correspondence business courses and public seminars. The Institute also offers an intensive three month program called The Entrepreneur Development Training Scheme for Malaysian Businessmen (sponsored by the Malaysian Government), the International Seminar on Japanese Business and Management which runs for five weeks, and the Executive Development Program for foreign managers of subsidiaries in Japan for one month.

Japan Management Association

This is a non-profit association of management consultants which has developed programs as demand has risen. The first courses were offered in the 1950s to deal with problems in industrial engineering and related activities. The Association offers short courses of between five and twelve days which are run several times a year, and certificates are awarded upon successful completion. Courses offered include the following which are usually attended by managers in the particular area of specialisation:

Course	Length	Level of Participant	Teaching Method
Top Management	8 days	Senior Executives	Case method, lecturers, seminars
Executive Development	12 days	Middle Managers	Case method, lecturers, business games
Office Management Seminar	6 days	Middle Managers	Lectures, workshops
Sales Management	5 days	Middle Managers	Case method, lectures
Market Research Application	6 days	Middle Managers	Case method, lectures
Production Control	5 days	Middle Managers	Case method, lectures, simulation
Inventory Control	6 days	Middle Managers	Case method, lectures, simulation
Preventive Maintenance	5 days	Middle Managers	Case method, lectures, simulation.

Central Japan Industries Association (CJIA): Junior Executive Academy

The CJIA was established in 1953 to provide managerial consultant services to members. The Central
Japan Institute of Industrial Management is an
affiliated body which offers courses to (a) men
about to take over the management of family businesses through its Junior Executive Academy, and
(b) a series of other courses for supervisory and
managerial personnel. The program offered by the
Academy is of one year duration, and the participants have a previous degree and are usually
between twenty and thirty years of age. The program
for this group examines the way to reform management and production systems, about 40 per cent of

the time is spent on field work where they study the operations of their own plants, as well as touring plants overseas. In 1986 the group visited technological exhibitions and plants in Hanover, Korea, USA, Taiwan and China. Teaching methods include case method, lectures, sensitivity training, business games, workshops, role-playing and simulation.

The courses run outside the Academy for management include such aspects as practical management planning, improvement of efficiency and clerical work, and a forum on ways to activate the organisation. Those for supervisory personnel are more in the TWI mould.

International University of Japan (IUJ): Graduate School

A more recent institution on the educational scene, IUJ enrolled its first students in the Master of Arts in International Relations program in 1983. Within two years it had enlarged its operations and, as of May 1985, had established The Center for Japan-US Relations and The Institute of Middle Eastern Studies, both of which are felt to be of vital importance to Japan. A minimum of two years' residency is required for the Master's degree, with a combination of basic courses, core courses, electives, and a thesis making up the curriculum. Basic courses include international relations, economics, and one choice from seven other courses in such areas as anthropology, social science and linguistics. The core courses, electives and optional courses may be selected from such topic groupings as International Politics, International Economics, International Management, Japanese Studies, North American Studies, East and Southeast Asian Studies, and Middle Eastern Studies. A wide variety of courses is available within each topic grouping. Competency in English, which they view more as an international rather than a foreign language, is also required, with achievement at an acceptable TOEFL (Teaching of English as a Foreign Language) level demanded.

While the university will admit up to one hundred suitably qualified students each year, the number is only approaching that now. Over 50 per cent of the students are sent by leading Japanese companies and organisations, and roughly one third of the remainder are non-Japanese.

Year	Japanese	Non-Japanese	Total
1983	41 (33)	15	56 (33)
1984	45 (42)	15	60 (42)
1985	55 (48)	20	75 (58)
1986	62 (55)	32	94 (55)

Figures in brackets indicate students sent by companies (IUJ Brochure)

Being the only graduate university in Japan, IUJ adds another dimension to the university run programs.

Institute for International Studies and Training (IIST)

Established in 1969, this graduate level institute is extremely significant for both business and government officials seeking expertise in the international field. The institute was established by an act of parliament in 1967, and the intended enrolment for the one year program was 120. This was achieved during the first few years but, in 1981, the student enrolments had dropped to 58.(23) One possible reason for this decline could be that, although the course is at postgraduate level, no degree is awarded. Since achieving a relationship with the American Graduate School of International Management in Arizona whereby the institute's program has been credited as the first year of a two-year Master of International Management program operated by the American school, numbers have risen.

IIST is supervised by the Ministry of International Trade and Industry (MITI), with a board of directors reflecting the views of industry, government and education establishments. The program includes courses in international business, area studies of selected countries, tours of Japan and a selected country, together with English and another foreign language.

As was stated earlier, many other worthwhile institutional programs are offered in Japan, whether at university graduate schools or in professional organisations. The ones discussed in detail do reflect the patterns which exist in most of the programs and also indicate the large number and diversity of short courses available. One final point should be made concerning university programs before examining in-house training. Firstly, when recruiting new employees, companies pay no more attention to a graduate in business administration than they would to a commerce, arts or science graduate. According to Ueno there is some justification for taking this approach, as many universities still emphasise abstract and theoretical matters rather than actual business practices and realities.(24) Employers tend to look upon graduates as high quality blank pages ready to be inscribed upon in a way which will benefit the company and the graduate.

The second point relates to graduate programs in management and business administration. Two patterns, the Keio Harvard influenced program and that operating at the International University of Japan, have been discussed with mention being made of some of their characteristics. If space permitted, a similar approach would be followed for all such programs, but it would rapidly become apparent that a great deal of similarity existed. For example, an examination of the programs at Sophia and Meiji Universities showed that, while the organisation of subjects might be different, and that one university might offer one or two different sounding courses, the majority of the courses were similar. Differences probably do exist in terms of the quality of staff and facilities, but these aspects are difficult to determine unless one has a close personal knowledge through experience of them. Therefore, and despite the reputation these institutions deservedly hold, and, as in the case of Sophia, the worldwide reputation it may have in research and publication, it is not intended to discuss additional graduate or undergraduate programs.

In-Company Training

The process of fitting new people into the constant flow of managerial personnel within an enterprise commences before the new employee joins the company. Great care is taken during the selection process with much more emphasis placed on level of education and personality characteristics than on specific subject knowledge and specific subject training. Sasaki(25) comments on the fact that while companies give a variety of exams and tests to applicants to test their knowledge and ability in liberal arts, languages and technical fields, more than 75 per cent of them make the interview more important than any other consideration. One survey published in 1974 showed that, when considering the relative importance of items at an interview, employers placed 88 per cent on character and personality, 10 per cent on looks and attitudes, 25.7 per cent on ability and knowledge, 77.1 per cent on ambition and aggressiveness, and 9.5 per cent on career and family environment.(26) By ensuring that the applicant's personal characteristics and ability fit well with company expectations and, therefore, with the group members with whom he will work, the company avoids bringing in someone who may cause problems for the company and himself. The ideal entrant would appear to be cooperative, ambitious within acceptable parameters, conscientious, loyal, and willing to fit in with company plans.

Once the graduate has joined the company, it places more emphasis on developing his managerial potential through job rotation and on-the-job training, than on outside educational programs. Subocz(27) suggests one reason for this might be that, although the courses have prestige value, they take the employee away from the group environment within which managerial potential is evaluated. Before discussing actual examples of company training programs, a brief discussion of the general pattern might be helpful. This description relates more to the early development of the graduate as he becomes inducted into the company, gains knowledge and work experience, and hopefully starts being identified as possible managerial material. It should be remembered that while all graduates had reasonable hopes for a management position during the high growth period in the 1960s, the growth rate has decreased rapidly since then and very few graduates currently achieve managerial positions.

In April of each year all new employees join the company and go through an introductory training period. Normally, the graduate intake receive a longer period of training with some companies, such as Toyota, classifying the entire first year as one of employee training. This usually takes the form of an orientation program where information about the company, its rules, mottoes and other aspects are discussed, then various periods of lectures, seminars, on-the-job training and job rotation occur. At the conclusion of this period the employee is given a job placement which could last from two to three years, or sometimes more. During this stage he is given jobs felt to be equal to his ability and he is observed as he carries out his duties. One aspect which appears fairly common in most companies and with which he must become conversant, is the 'ringi' system of decision-making. With this system, when a new idea, plan, or suggestion for change arises, it is first discussed at length within the group from whence it came. When consensus has been achieved within this group it extends laterally to other groups for discussion and evaluation and, if agreement is reached, the proposal starts to move up the organisational ladder where it once again is discussed and approved or otherwise. By the time a successful proposal reaches the top it has been through virtually all the groups, sections and departments with which it is associated. This involves group members in such activities as negotiating, discussing, developing their ideas within the group and, later, with the possibility of demonstrating their initiative in the planning for implementation of the proposal. Not only does this give each group member the opportunity to develop and demonstrate his ability in these roles, but also gives him the chance to be 'noticed' by his peers and superiors. Morita(28) states that industry expects that graduates should have an advantage in this process as their education should provide them with: (a) ability to formulate their own approach, (b) the ability to cope with and solve problems arising unexpectedly, and (c) the ability to make lucid analysis and evaluation. Dickerman(29) supported this conclusion when he said that the principles of systematic thinking learned at university should make them well qualified to analyse and solve managerial problems.

Job rotation also adds to the development of the potential manager in that he not only gains knowledge and experience in many aspects of the company's operations, but also gets to know personnel in other sections of the company. The more capable a managerial prospect appears to be, the more opportunities he will be given to gain experience by placing him in a wider variety of jobs. While the majority of graduates being evaluated would move through the system at about the same rate, more capable performers move at an accelerated pace as they are recognised and prepared for roles in top management. During this period of rotation the company decides which people it wishes to develop into specialists and who shall be generalists. The longer an employee stays in one position the more specialised he becomes and the opportunities for gaining a variety of experience are lost. As general consensus among management favours the promotion of generalists to top management, decisions about individual appointments can be crucial. Sasaki(30) suggests that, as the potential manager moves up the seniority ladder, he gains both knowledge and supervisory experience in a variety of sections within several departments. 'After his rotation finishes, he continues his development in one department while digesting his various experiences. By the time he reaches top management level, he should be a generalist. Of course the smaller the area of rotation, the more of a specialist capacity he acquires. The length of stay in any given position is usually no longer than three years.'

A series of interviews with a range of Japanese companies was carried out by the writer during 1978, 1979 and 1983. Companies such as Kawasaki Heavy Industries, Nippon Electric Company (NEC), Sony, Matsushita Electric, Nippon Telephone and Telegraph, Toyota, Nissan, and Teijin Textiles were included in this survey which concerned the selection processes employed by the personnel departments when recruiting new employees, and the training programs provided for both blue collar workers and for future managerial personnel. With slight variations in activities and emphases the pattern described in the above section appeared to be common to all. However, as the potential managers began to be recognised, the companies began to supplement the training received through job rotation and on-the-job training by selecting a number of them to participate in formal training programs. While it is clear that some companies, particularly the small and middle sized ones, utilise the services of such groups as SANNO, Japan Productivity Centre and the Japan Management Association, the larger corporations have their own training staff and facilities and the majority of training programs are internal. Several of the companies which were interviewed have been selected, and a brief discussion of their programs will now be conducted.

Teijin (Textiles) Limited

The company, which was established in 1918, was

involved mainly in producing rayon until 1957. Systems of TWI and MTP were introduced into the company following the establishment of an education section in the Iwakuni and Mihara plants in 1949. In 1960, in order 'to reform the old style of management' the company president issued two papers - 'Guidelines for the Conduct of Company Employees' and 'Principles for Guiding Subordinates'. Following these statements, courses were conducted for all company managers. Included in these courses were:

> Management Training Course (MTP)
> Training in the Setting of Goals and
>   Determination of Policy
> Quality Control Training
> Creative Thinking Course

Other courses such as 'Guidelines for the Development of Ideas' were also developed, as were computer familiarity courses.

> The present goal of personnel development is to enable employees to adapt to current trends in internationalisation and diversification of our business. The basis of personnel development lies in on-the-job training which emphasises <u>self development</u>. It is therefore necessary to systemise the cycle of self appraisal, education, personnel evaluation, incentive and reward programs, and job rotation in order to maximise employee development.(31)

The program in 1979 included the following:

1. Lectures and discussion for managers.
2. Management training for staff members.
   (a) How to train employees on the job
   (b) Managerial grid seminars
   (c) How to train employees by the TWI method
   (d) Communication seminars.
3. Foreman training.
4. Group leader training.
5. Technical training for plant workers.
6. Training in quality control.
7. Orientation training for new employees.

The total number of employees in this company is about 7,200, and they are divided between Tokyo and Osaka headquarters and six plants.

Number of Employees by Category

Plant	White Collar		Blue Collar		
	Above sub-dept manager	Others	Foreman	Others	Total
Iwakuni (fibre)	15	49	45	241	350
Mihara (fibre)	27	90	96	864	1077
Matsuyama (fibre)	68	200	174	1737	2179
Tokuyama (fibre)	12	48	43	253	356
Ehime (fibre)	17	68	51	465	601
Gifu (fibre)	11	53	35	267	366

Upon joining the company the graduates receive a one-week orientation program followed by a two month training program. In the first week they are acquainted with such information as knowledge about the company, company rules and company structure. During the next month they work with process workers in the plants to get to know the processes used, as well as to develop a good attitude towards working in the company. The final three weeks are spent gaining information concerning such activities as sales, company filing procedures, and how to conduct group discussions. They are then allocated to a particular plant to start on-the-job training for approximately three years.

As can be seen from the above table the number of managerial personnel who at various times are engaged in training activities designed by the company is quite considerable.

In addition to the formal activities already mentioned, there is an information on-going program of personnel development in which, at some stage of their career at Teijin, each employee participates. A simplified presentation of this approach might be shown as follows:

SELF APPRAISAL	GOAL SETTING	INCENTIVE & REWARDS	OBJECTIVES
Review of performance	Coaching by a superior	Promotion	To strengthen manpower ability
Self evaluation of ability	Coaching by staff of Personnel Department	Job rotation	To use talents effectively
Area to which one would like to be placed		Education & training	To achieve and maintain company profits
Morale survey			To promote and rotate employees by assessment of performance and not on seniority

The emphasis on self development included in the statement by Teijin was reflected in comments by most of the companies interviewed and was also mentioned by Dickerman.(32) He quoted the results of a survey of 855 Japanese firms carried out by the Japan Industrial Training Association in 1971, which showed a variety of self development approaches being followed by those firms.

1. Inquiry and agency services for extramural courses and seminars, 62 per cent.
2. Distribution of teaching texts and other materials for self development, 45 per cent.
3. Preparation and distribution of lists of recommended publications, 33 per cent.
4. Provision for courses and seminars on an optional basis, 27 per cent.
5. Economic support for voluntary groups for self development, 27 per cent.
6. Service for voluntary training groups, 22 per cent.

The more recent comments by Teijin and other firms indicate that the self development activities are still being encouraged.

Matsushita Electric Industrial Company

The Matsushita empire commenced its operations in 1918 when the founder, Konosuke Matsushita developed a double outlet adapter to fit into electric light sockets, thus doubling their capacity. Since then such company brands as Pioneer, National and Panasonic have become known worldwide for the quality and range of their products. One of the major reasons given for this by managerial personnel is the extremely comprehensive company training programs which stimulate, upgrade and retain personnel at all levels. As the number of products manufactured by the company increased in the 1930s, Matsushita introduced a company-wide program of job rotation. Under this program 5 per cent of employees, comprised equally of managers, supervisors and workers, were rotated to new departments each year. Since that time the company has extended, developed and refined the training program and, in the process, has developed outstanding training facilities.

Initial training for university and college graduates consists of one month orientation in much the same manner as described for Teijin. The three months following this are spent in retail shops throughout Japan, assisting in sales, learning why particular items sell, what customers want or expect, and other activities of a similar nature. Following this period, trainees spend the next four months in different manufacturing departments where they work in the process line, learning how the products are made and actually making, assembling and testing. Upon completion of this eight month period the non-science graduates are placed in their first positions and commence work. Science graduates, however, spend an additional four months in manufacturing to determine where their particular area of specialisation might be. As the company was employing approximately 400 new graduates each year in the 1970s (500 in 1978; 450 in 1977), it is clear that both a large training staff and a well co-ordinated program would be required.

The range of programs available for managerial personnel is extremely wide, covering such areas as supervisory staff, engineering management, production management and general administration management.

Manufacturing Management Course	Production Planning, Cost Analysis, Line Control, Quality Control, Work Improvements
Service Management Course	Parts Control, Service Shop Management, Claim Information, Technical Seminars
Sales Management Course	Sales Strategy, Planning, Promotion, Merchandising, Business Analysis
Accounting Management Course	Management Systems, Business Planning, Financial Statement Analysis, Cost Analysis and Management
Personnel Management Course	Personnel Principles, Recruiting, Appointment and Rotation, Labor Relations, Education and Training
International Trade Course	Triangular Trade, Foreign Exchange, Finance, Distribution
Director Course	Discussions with Matsushita's Executive, Case Studies

All courses 10 days duration

If the above program were used as an example of similar programs in production or engineering management, then some idea of the programs for potential and current managers can be obtained. The engineering management program, for instance, has twenty-five courses ranging through quality control to creativity in developing new ideas, human relations, cost control and industrial design. The number of personnel in the courses ranges from twenty to thirty, and the courses last from one to ten days.

ACHIEVEMENTS IN MANAGEMENT EDUCATION

Having looked at changes in the field of management education, whether within a company or available through programs offered by academic or professional institutes, it should now be possible to determine what, if anything, has been achieved. Many managerial approaches, such as paternalism, which are being perceived as becoming increasingly less effective and more expensive, still persist in varying degrees in many companies. Other practices, linked to either the pre-Meiji merchant houses, such as familial style relationships, or to early modernisation practices like the labour-stabilising role of pay scales based on seniority, may also still be found in most companies. If these characteristics are used to infer that the training and education given to managers has been ineffective and a waste of time, then an incorrect conclusion has been drawn. Although these practices may still exist in Japanese companies, new managerial practices and a shrinking growth rate are putting all of these characteristics, including lifetime employment, under increasing threat and their effective removal from the scene would appear to be imminent. Instead of looking at the persistence of pre-modern practices, why not examine the positive results of the management education programs?

In 1956 the Keizai Doyukai emphasised the need for the training of future managers by systematic programs of development. The joint Time-Life and International Management Association of Japan study tour of North America and Europe in 1973 proposed that specialised modern managerial education programs, whether based on Western, Japanese, or a combination of the best features from both, should be instituted in Japan as rapidly as possible. As can be seen from the chronology, at the times these statements were made the programs available within the company or in outside institutes were very limited. The large range of short and long courses and programs offered by both professional agencies and academic institutions demonstrates quite forcibly that appropriate bodies have responded to the expressed needs of industry and commerce. Companies have also responded by increasing the nature and range of programs within the company for potential and existing managers or, where it was felt to be more efficient or appropriate, have either brought in outside educators or sent personnel to programs offered by the professional or academic institutes. If these programs were not meeting the needs of industry and commerce, company and individual support would cease and the institutes offering them would be in financial difficulties. The institutes realise this only too well, and a close liaison between the training bodies and companies is maintained. As the professional bodies offering programs frequently are engaged in consultancy work with the companies, rapid and flexible responses to company needs can be achieved.

Training programs within companies also reflect modern managerial education influences. While emphasis is placed on successful Japanese managerial training such as job rotation and the ringi system of decision making, Western influences in the form of courses utilising simulation, case study approach, syndicate work and group discussions appear consistently in company programs. A common theme pushed by those companies interviewed, and appearing in articles by commentators on Japanese management education, is that in the majority of cases both companies and individuals, for the reasons stated earlier in the chapter, prefer the training to be carried out within the company rather than being separated from the company while engaged in the training program. Smaller firms generally have little choice but to utilise the courses offered by the various training institutes to supplement the job rotation, ringi system and self development programs which can be operated within the firm.

The current international status of Japanese managerial techniques is not only a positive affirmation of the value of the managerial training programs, but has stimulated an intense interest in Western nations. The high quality of Japanese products resulting from such programs as the quality control circle and zero defects program, illustrates the effectiveness of the way in which management has harnessed the energy and creativeness of its work force.

While training bodies introduce and develop courses to enhance the growth and development of employees, the pragmatic Japanese decision-makers will support them and their efforts. In an endeavour to gain more student and, possibly, company support, some training institutes have rushed into offering the latest courses from America and Europe without ensuring sufficient preparation and knowledge on the part of the instructor. This has resulted in the criticism that some courses were of questionable standards, suffering from poor quality of instruction and often attempting to capitalise on the 'newness' of a course and to ignore basics.(33)

Future developments in management education are closely related to the economy. Japan has demonstrated over a period of centuries that it looks to education to meet its short and long-term needs. The deliberate introduction of Confucian education by Tokugawa Ieyasu in the 1600s as a means of pacifying the warring samurai, and the manner in which the Japanese government, between 1890 and 1945, manipulated and indoctrinated the population through the discriminate changes in moral lessons to prepare for industrial growth or war as the situation changed, ably demonstrate this approach. As the industrial economy changes and the company is faced with new problems and challenges, it would be out of character not to look to education to shape management and the work force to meet them. The current slow-down in growth and high value of the yen is affecting Japan's export markets drastically. Already one of the tenets of Japan's company policy - lifetime employment - is under threat. How company management will cope with this is not clear at this stage. The government may move in as it did during the Oil Shock of the 1970s and come to an agreement with employers and unions on a tripartite mutual support and subsidy system; then again it may not. Whatever the future holds, however, it is extremely probably that management education will be utilised to achieve the desired goal.

NOTES

1. A. Dickerman, Training Japanese Managers, Praeger Publishers, New York, (1984), p.4.
2. M.Y. Yoshino, Japan's Managerial System: Tradition and Innovation, MIT Press, Massachusetts, 1968, p.22.
3. R.P. Dore, Education in Tokugawa Japan, Routledge and Kegan Paul, London, 1965, p.305.
4. Yoshino, p.124.
5. W. Lockwood (ed.), The State and Economic Enterprise in Japan, Princeton University Press, 1965, p.448.
6. C. Johnson, MITI and the Japanese Miracle, Stanford University Press, Stanford, 1982, p.31.
7. Dickerman, p.23.
8. Yoshino, p.96.
9. S. Takamiya, 'Development of Japanese Management', Management Japan, Vol.16, No.1, Spring 1983, p.11.
10. Yoshino, p.102.
11. Yoshino, p.111.
12. International Management Association of Japan (IMAJ). 'Lessons Learned from Western Managerial Training Programs', Management Japan, Vol.7, Nos. 2 & 3, 1974.
13. Dickerman, p.24.
14. N.G. McNulty, Training Managers: The International Guide, Harper and Row, New York, 1969 and Management Development Programs: The World's Best, North-Holland, Amsterdam, 1980.
15. V. Subocz, 'Management Education in Japan: Extent, Directions and Problems', Journal of Management Development, Vol.3, No.4, 1984.
16. R. Clark, The Japanese Company, Yale University Press, New Haven, 1979, p.17.
17. I. Ueno, 'The Situation of Management Education in Japan', Management Education, OECD, Paris, 1972, p.37.
18. Yoshino, p.243.
19. Yoshino, p.244.
20. R.J. Ballon, 'Top Executives and Company Presidents in Japan: Function and Personality'. Bulletin No. 27, Sophia University Socio-Economic Institute, Tokyo, 1971, pp.7-8.
21. Subocz, p.31.
22. Japan Productivity Center, Productivity Movement in Japan, 1986, p.13.
23. Subocz, p.36.
24. Ueno, p.39.

25. N. Sasaki, Management and Industrial Structure in Japan, Pergamon Press, Great Britain, 1981, p.2.

26. Sasaki, p.32. (Note: Employers were able to make multiple responses to list of characteristics desired in applicants).

27. Subocz, p.23.

28. A. Merita, 'The Situation of Management Education in Japan', Management Education, OECD, Paris, 1972, p.89.

29. Dickerman, p.24.

30. Sasaki, p.34.

31. Teijin Limited. Outline of Educational and Training Programs at Teijin, p.2.

32. Dickerman, p.85.

33. Subocz, p.31.

Chapter Nine

CONCLUSION: ACHIEVEMENTS AND THE FUTURE
William Byrt

It will be seen from the preceding chapters that it
is difficult to identify one, homogeneous concept
which may be termed management education. Methods
of improving the performance of managers, whether
called management education or management training,
vary from one country to another. Within each
country, they vary in their organisation, methods,
teachers and taught.

There has been a tendency in English-speaking
countries to except as the typical model of
management education one based on the United States
experience, particularly that of the Harvard
Business School. However, other countries have not
always followed the US model. Some that have done
so originally have subsequently modified their
approaches to meet local needs and to take account
of local conditions.

In many cases, methods of management education
have been adapted and their use expanded without
any critical assessment of need or appraisal of
results. Inquiries such as those of Cyert and Ralph
in Australia, and similar inquiries in other
countries, have been concerned more with funding,
organisation and staffing than with need or
results. In Australia, in my own State of Victoria,
management education courses offered by certain
tertiary institutions are, before being accredited,
examined by committees. This examination
concentrates on funding, organisation, staffing,
content and demand (sometimes, one suspects,
stimulated by judicious lobbying) rather than on
need or results.

So what has been achieved by means of management education and what appears to be its future? One is making judgments here as hard data in support of conclusions are hard to come by.

Shakespeare had Mark Anthony proclaim over the body of Caesar:

'The evil that men do lives after them,
The good is oft interred with their bones'.

It is easier to uncover criticisms than conclusive evidence of results of a practice such as management education. Critics tend to be vocal and persistent and to indulge in sweeping generalisations. Supporters take the line that, if so many students wish to undertake courses and so many courses are offered, they <u>must</u> be good! Accordingly, I will start by considering some of the more common criticisms, in some cases condemnations, of management education.

CRITICISMS

Most of the criticisms levelled at management education are directed at the award courses, although the non-award, short courses also come under fire from time to time.

The major criticisms are of its:

Organisation
Content
Method
Product.

Organisation

A good deal of management education is carried out within tertiary education institutions. The reasons for this are obvious. Education in various forms is the business of such institutions. They are staffed by professional educators. They are able to provide facilities such as classrooms and libraries. They can develop a research-base as a foundation to their teaching.

The criticisms have been many, however. Most teaching institutions are bureaucratically managed and it has been alleged that their dominant cultures are inimical to efficient management. Management or business schools are not shining

211

examples of efficiency within the institutions of which they are a part. Frequently, they attract as staff people more interested in teaching and research, even in the quiet life, than in management: 'Those who can do; those who can't teach'.

In fairness, it must be said that tertiary institutions around the world are moving away from being quiet havens of contemplation and security, characterised by dreaming spires and lost causes, which, it is alleged, they once were or aimed to be. Contract employment, appointment and promotion based on assessed performance and the encouragement of entrepreneurial activities designed to attract funds are becoming common.

It has been said that educational institutions are the only ones where knowledge is placed in packages - faculties, departments, degrees,subjects - with labels and boundaries. Most award courses in management education are made up of a number of subjects, taught in prescribed terms or seminars, assessment being made through conventional, formalised methods. Schools providing the courses are part of larger educational institutions, subject to the bureaucratic rules and regulations of the latter. It is only recently, in the case of some of the management schools, that they have been able to obtain their independence from the faculties in which they were established - usually Economics or Accounting - and obtained some recognition as providers of a distinct, respectable academic discipline.

Many management schools have been accused of being too far removed from business, which constitutes their constituency, the source of material on which to base teaching and research and the market for their product, their graduates. The same criticisms are, of course, levelled at other faculties, such as those of Medicine, Law, Engineering, Education.

Management schools have tried to close the gap between them and business in a number of ways. Provision of consultancy services to industry; action-research projects; use, for teaching purposes, of case-studies based on actual situations in industry; interchange of staff with industry; appointment of staff, on either a full or part-time basis, of persons with experience in management. However, in many institutions, most persons, in order to secure appointment to or promotion in academic positions, must follow the conventional academic track of research, doctorate, publications. Accordingly, there is an increasing tendency for staff to be in-bred and 'academic'. The practices outlined earlier in this paragraph are seen largely as expedients, as palliatives.

Identical criticisms are not levelled at short, non-award courses, either external or in-house. However, there have been a variety of other criticisms, varying from situation to situation:

> External short courses do not meet the specific needs of particular undertakings.

> What is taught on both external and in-house courses is not translated back to the work-place.

> Many courses are not well-designed or organised.

> Teaching tends to be of a varied quality.

> The longer courses, four weeks or more, include a good deal of 'padding' and result in participants being away from their jobs for an excessively long period.

Some management education is, of course, provided outside tertiary educational institutions. However, most of these lack the prestige, staff and facilities of the latter. It is not uncommon for some of them to seek affiliation or closer relationship with universities or colleges. Thus, in Great Britain in 1972, Henley: The Management College formed a link with Brunel University.

Content

Early management education courses had a fairly solid basis of economics - management was considered to be of economic institutions - to which was later added accounting, then behavioural science and, later still, quantitative methods of analysis and decision-making.

There is little agreement on what subjects should constitute a management training or education course. There is a good deal of similarity between the offerings of various institutions. However, this would appear to be more a result of copying foreign and local models and to similarities in the backgrounds of those constructing and

213

teaching courses, rather than to any systematic assessment of the needs of the participants and of the industries in which they are employed. A four-fold classification of subjects commonly offered may be made: Basic Disciplines; Environmental Analyses; Management Functions; Management Skills.

Basic Disciplines	Environmental Analyses
Accounting	Banking
Business Law	Business/Government
Economics	Relationships
Industrial Law	Environment
Management Theory	Economic
Mathematics	Political
Organisational Behaviour	Social
Organisational Theory	Financial Markets
Sociology	International Business
	Public Administration

Management Functions	Management Skills
Corporate Planning	Advertising
Finance	Communication
Human Resource	Computing
Management	Entrepreneurship
Industrial Relations	Financial Analysis
Investment Management	Forecasting
Leadership	Market Research
Marketing	Motivation
Operations Management	Negotiation
Organisational	Operations Research
Management	Problem Solving
Organisational Design	Quantitative Analysis
Product Management	
Project Management	
Strategy Formulation	
Systems Design &	
Analysis	

The content of a particular course probably depends on a variety of factors: the history of the development of the course; current fads; the culture of the organisation within which the course is conducted; expressed preferences of influential clients; the interests of key faculty members.

The relevance of subjects making up the content of any course will depend partly on how well they are taught and partly on what the student hopes to gain from them.

A well-taught subject, even if not directly
relevant to the vocational interests of students,
may stimulate them so that their analytical
faculties are developed and intellectual horizons
widened. A recurrent criticism of management
education courses, as of many others offered by
tertiary institutions, are that they are not well-
taught. That teachers are more interested in
research, administration or consultancy than they
are in teaching. A questionnaire issued to students
at an Australian university elicited the following
two comments, among many others:

> 'Many academics do not like teaching and
> do not bother to hide the fact.'

> 'Mr... (the lecturer) exhibits a real
> interest in his subject which is most
> unusual among academics.'

Some business schools are placing greater emphasis
on teaching although, usually, it rates below
research and publications in the ranking of
criteria to be taken into account for the purposes
of appointment or promotion. Many schools have,
over a long period, asked students to rate their
teachers; a practice which originated in the United
States. A criticism of this 'popularity poll' has
been that it has led some teachers to 'play up' to
their students, to adopt the roles of entertainers
rather than educators.
    It does appear that most students attending
management education courses seek training rather
than education. They wish to be trained in skills
which will help them further their careers.
Accordingly, their rating of subjects in terms of
relevance depends largely on the extent to which
they see such subjects assisting them to attain
this objective. Increasing emphasis is being given
to mathematically-based subjects and to finance,
areas in which many students are not proficient and
which they see as being essential in today's business environment. Some observers have been critical
of what they see as the comparative neglect of
important areas such as organisational behaviour,
industrial relations, business/government relationships and the cross-cultural study of management.

Conclusion: Achievements and the Future

Method

Teaching methods used in management education vary. There is, however, a good deal of reliance on experiential methods, those drawing on the experience of participants rather than on text-books or lectures.

Most business schools, particularly those developed according to the US Model, make use of the so-called 'Harvard case-study method', which may be regarded as management education's major pedagogical contribution.

The use of case-studies in management education can be effective, depending on the skill of the teacher, the relevance of the case-study used and the willingness and ability of members of the class to participate. A 'good' case-study is usually based on an actual situation and should be designed to evoke responses from the class based on their own experiences. The method simulates situations likely to be encountered by managers in their work. Also, it encourages group decision-making.

There are, however, critics of the case-study method, the major criticisms being:

A 'class-room response' may be evoked. Decisions reached by students in analysing a case-study may not be the same as those which they would make in real situations. It is easy to stand-off and pontificate about matters which do not affect one.

Despite the fact that the method is often described as 'participatory' or 'democratic', the study of cases is, in many instances, dominated by the teacher.(1)

There is a shortage of 'good' case-studies. Academics do not get as much credit for writing cases as they do for having articles published in refereed journals. Accordingly, some case-studies become over-used and 'standard answers' are handed on from class to class.

Management education suffers from a lack of up-to-date research base. Much of it is based on folk-lore, the untested theories of 'practical men' or research carried out decades ago. The latter, in some cases, might not stand up to rigorous testing, has been accepted uncritically, too much has been claimed for it or it is of doubtful relevance under today's conditions.

Most modern research into management is not carried out in research institutes but by academics, individually or in twos or threes. It complements their teaching and often seems designed more to impress appointment and promotion committees and their colleagues, rather than to expand the frontiers of knowledge. It is published in refereed journals for a select few, both the organ of publication and the style of writing ensuring that it will not be read by a larger audience. Many of the researchers are:

'...fact-collectors, scholar-squirrels for whom every season's May'.(2)

They play

'games that must played in order for them to rise in the academic bureaucracy'.(3)

Product

It has been claimed in a number of countries that MBA graduates have placed excessively high 'price-tickets' on themselves and that their inflated evaluations have been accepted uncritically by some employers. On the other hand, some MBAs consider that employers expect too much of them and become disillusioned and critical when they cannot solve deep-rooted problems which have defied the efforts of experienced managers for many years.

Postgraduate programs in management education tend to attract, as students, ambitious people, looking to change their career paths, who place a good deal of value on credentialism, the possession of paper-qualifications. They may or may not prove to be effective managers.

A criticism of such programs is that they are more effective in developing the analytical skills of students than their operational skills, their abilities to implement plans, to get things done. There is an apocryphal story of the Baker Scholar, one of the top group graduating MBA from Harvard, who was employed, without success, in the Production, Finance, Marketing and Personnel Departments of the corporation which had hired him upon graduation. When asked if he could suggest a department in which he could be employed productively, he answered:

'Have you a case-study, department? I'm good at doing them.'

Many MBA graduates, shortly after graduation, take up positions the main function of which is financial analysis. Is this management?

Management education, particularly the MBA, constitutes something of educational 'Aunt Sally' at which critics, from time-to-time, fire missiles. It has been attacked as emphasising an elitist philosophy of education which runs counter to current trends in society:

'The idea of producing a group of young wiz kid managers who will be conditioned decision-makers is not only an out-dated, but dangerous concept.

In a society where there is an increasing demand for participation at all levels it is simply unrealistic to adopt what Professor Leonard Sayles of Columbia University has so aptly described as the war-room approach to management education.

Such an approach assumes that a group of trained decision-makers sitting in a war room (or board room) can make the appropriate or correct trade-offs provided they have adequate information systems.

'War-room' is a doubly appropriate expression when one looks at the disasters and blunders of the US and Australian involvement in Vietnam. That war was planned and waged with American access to the most sophisticated technology, computerised data and the highest managerial expertise.

The former US Secretary of Defence, Mr. Robert McNamara, was once a top Ford executive. Yet, nearly every decision of the war-room carried with it the seeds of further disaster until defeat of US war aims became inevitable.

One has only to look at the way local groups are emerging to challenge and

counter-plan against the decisions of
State and local government planners to see
that authoritarian decision-making is no
longer acceptable in our community'.(4)

Criticism of business schools is not confined to
the political left, although Marxists have attacked
them on the grounds that they tend to recruit
conservative staff, provide support for the values
of capitalism and solicit, and in some cases
obtain, fairly substantial funds from business.

Barbara Tuchman places a fair share of the
blame for the United States debacle in Vietnam on
Robert McNamara:

'... a prodigy of the Harvard Business
School, of 'systems analysis' for the Air
Force during World War II and of rapid
rise afterwards to the presidency of the
Ford Motor Company... McNamara was a
specialist of management through 'statistical control'... Anything that could be
quantified was his realm. ... he had the
ruthlessness of uninterrupted success, and
his genius for statistics left little
respect for human variables and no room
for unpredictables'.(5)

The 'Australian Financial Review' of 26 June, 1979,
considered the annual report of Derek Bok,
President of Harvard University, in which he
criticised the Harvard Business School's teaching
methods, particularly the case study approach,
research capabilities and preparation of students
for new and complex business problems.

'Time' of 4 May 1981, contained a cover story
entitled 'The Money Chase: Business School
Solutions May be Part of the US Problem'. Among
the criticisms made were that:

. MBA graduates are expensive, arrogant and lack
  loyalty.
. A lot of what is preached at business schools
  is 'absolute rot'
. Students are taught that quite serious business
  problems can be solved by comparatively brief
  analyses.
. The methods of analysis are biased towards the
  short-term.

Conclusion: Achievements and the Future

An article in 'The Wall Street Journal' of 11 October 1985, commented on MBA graduates':

> '...immaturity and lack of work experience with... inflated sense of their own skills, potential and ability'.

The criticisms quoted refer to American business schools. However, many schools outside the USA are patterned on American models, the younger academics see American methods as laudable and academics from the United States are welcomed.

A survey of employer attitudes to MBA courses conducted by Professor Chris Orpen of Deakin University, in Victoria, Australia, found among other things:

. Most managers felt MBA courses should try to improve practical managerial skills rather than analytic and quantitative skills.
. They regarded areas requiring judgment, such as marketing, human resources and strategic planning, as more important than technical areas like quantitative methods and accounting.
. They thought the courses focused too much on 'ivory tower' concepts, and favoured the use of case studies and should be 'teaching-oriented as opposed to a research-oriented faculty to improve MBA programs'.

ACHIEVEMENTS

The preceding section may appear to constitute a fairly lengthy indictment of management education and one may be tempted to ask, with little Peterkin:

> 'But what good came of it at last'. (6)

However, management education has spread in a variety of forms in many countries. It has done so despite a comparative lack of an intellectual, philosophical or research base, the antagonism of academics in established disciplines and, in many cases, paucity of resources. One does not need to be a Social Darwinist to take the view that, essentially, it must have been fit to survive.

The list of criticisms is lengthy but it must be said that each critic would not necessarily accept all, or even most of the criticisms. Critics

are stimulated to attack because of their own
interests, prejudices or values: the need which
they feel to defend their own position; sheer
conservatism: 'We've got by without management
education for centuries': their ideology - some
management theorists have been labeled the
'servants of power'(7); unfortunate experiences
with brash products of management-education
courses; disenchantment because such courses have
not had the results which <u>they</u> considered that they
should have, which might never have been promised
by management educators.

Despite the criticisms, management education
has had its achievements and is a growth-industry
in many countries. What <u>has</u> been achieved? This is
a difficult question to answer as is the same
question when posed about the effects of many other
systems of education and training. Is the community
better served by having pharmacists, nurses, archi-
tects and accountants produced through degree
courses rather than through forms of apprenticeship
supplemented by some part-time study?

Assessment of the results of management
education activities is usually made by tracing the
careers of those who have undertaken courses,
particularly the MBA, by making judgments about the
standard of management in organisations and by
asking those who have completed courses whether or
not they have benefited from them.

Most of the evidence is satisfying to management educators but still inconclusive. A large
number of persons who have obtained top management
positions have undergone management education.
However, many top managers have not done so. Would
the former have risen to the top in any case?

The quality of management in most of the
countries considered earlier is probably superior
to what it was, say, twenty or thirty years ago.
However, to what extent is this due to management
education and training and to what extent a result
of technological advances, the easier flow of
information between countries, which of course has
as one of its channels management education, and
the higher general level of education of the
community?

<u>Most</u> persons who have undertaken management
education or training state that they have benefited from it. Some claim that they have not or
that it only confirmed what they already knew.
Those who discern benefits may, of course, be
looking back through rose-tinted glasses on an

experience which, at the time, they did not enjoy or about which they had doubts. Having completed the course, they may feel that they have a vested interest in upholding its values; this gives them an advantage over others who have not undertaken the course.

On the other hand, critics may not be being objective but reacting against an experience which they did not enjoy at the time, which interfered with their family, social or business lives and which they resented being forced by their employers to experience.

Positive achievements of management education may probably be summarised as being:

Facilitating the recognition of the 'business' aspect of many activities. Those in government departments and authorities, hospitals, professional practices, sporting bodies, churches, schools, universities. This has been termed a change from administration to management.

Permitting people who had made an inappropriate first-choice of career, or who had had such a choice thrust on them, to make a change.

Inducing an awareness of the managerial component of their roles on the part of people who had come to regard their positions as purely operative, technical or professional.

Gaining acceptance of the view that, although 'you only learn to manage by managing', one's managerial skills may be developed by means of training and education; just as one's ability at a sport may be developed by means of coaching.

THE FUTURE

In twenty years time it may be possible to make a reasonably accurate assessment of the results of management education in the countries surveyed. At present, the evidence is not conclusive and we are faced with biased, and sometimes emotional, critics and biased, and perhaps self-interested, defenders.

What are likely to be the directions taken by management education during the next two decades? One can only make predictions which may or may not be borne out.

Management education will probably continue to be given largely by postgraduate award courses, executive programs offered by educational institutions and consultants and in-house programs. Some may continue to be provided as part of undergraduate degree, diploma and certificate courses, but, in such cases, probably as an extra or 'icing on the cake'.

The greatest growth will probably be in in-house courses followed by external executive programs. If this growth does not occur, it will most likely be because of economic conditions and will constitute something of a test of top management's real commitment to, and belief in the value of, management education.

There will probably still be a demand for postgraduate qualifications, particularly from the ambitious, looking for credentials to boost their ambitions, and those wishing to change their career paths.

A major re-assessment of the offerings of educational institutions, both in award and non-award courses, is desirable. In the past, many courses were not so much developed as taken over from the United States with some local improvisation over time. The challenges of the remainder of this century require a realistic tailoring of courses, subjects and teaching methods.

Award courses should also, of course, be scrutinised critically in terms of structure, content and teaching methods. Debates about course structure and content will probably still continue. There is probably room for variations and experimentation in both as between educational establishments.

Leaving aside the arguments over 'hard' (quantitative) versus 'soft' (non-quantitative) subjects and theory versus practice, basically management education has, as its objectives: the development of students' analytical and critical judgment; understanding of the management of people, money, markets and production; understanding of industry's economic, political and social environments.

The better courses have achieved <u>some</u> success in each of these objectives. There has, perhaps, been too great a reliance on the case-study method

223

as means of developing the student's judgment. The value and shortcomings of this method were considered earlier.

The management of production has been neglected. Reasonable attention has been given to the management of people and of markets. However, there has been a tendency to accentuate the importance of financial management. Possibly because, in many countries, an expertise in this area appears to provide greater access to the 'glittering prizes' than do the other forms of management. Is there a temptation for the MBA graduate to become skilled in playing 'the money game', in company or financial institutions, rather than to become a manager of resources so as to produce goods and services?

The study of the economy still forms a major part of most management education programs. However, the study of the political and social environment has been neglected in many cases.

Today it is being asked: 'Do we expect too much of government?' Politicians, ranging from the left to the right, are concerned about big government, its cost and inability to achieve its objectives. The question might also be asked: 'Do we expect too much of management?' Different schools of critics blame different groups for the ills which have befallen developed countries: the trade unions; inept politicians; greedy consumers; the young who have abandoned the work ethic; managers. All must take their share of the blame, but where does remedial action start and what use is action in one area without it in the others?

There can be little doubt that more efficient and effective management can make some contribution to the solution of economic ills. However, to what extent is management education likely to contribute to the production of better managers? It can teach skills, broaden horizons and provide those undertaking it with imagination and credentials necessary to change career paths. It is unlikely to breed entrepreneurs, in fact, in some cases it may inhibit the development of entrepreneurial ability. It does not provide a nostrum for all economic ills. More importantly, as management educators are divided about what they should be teaching and what should be taught, are they the best persons to teach it?

One final point. In a number of countries, for example the United States, Great Britain, Canada, Australia, we are witnessing a growth in 'educational imperialism'; the export of education, including that in management, to non-western countries. Two questions may be posed:

Is this motivated more by a desire to profit than to spread the gospel?

Is the gospel appropriate to the needs of such countries?

NOTES

1.   Chris Argyris, 'Some Limitations of the Case Method; Experiences in a Management Development Program', Academy of Management Review (1980) Vol.5, No.2, pp.291-8.

2.   Gore Vidal, The Second American Revolution and Other Essays (1976-1982), Random House, New York, (1982), p.12.

3.   Ibid, p.35.

4.   Clyde Cameron, 'The Australian Financial Review', September 4 (1973), p.3.

5.   Barbara Tuckman, The March of Folly, Abacus, London (1985), p.355.

6.   Robert Southey, 'The Battle of Blenheim'.

7.   Loren Baritz, The Servants of Power, John Wiley & Sons, New York (1965).

Index